signature
pasta

Italian Cooking & Living

signature pasta

**America's 26 top chefs
share their best pasta recipes**

Paolo VILLORESI & Micol NEGRIN
Food Photography Jerry RUOTOLO

The Italian Table

Text copyright © 2000 by The Italian Table

All photographs copyright © 2000 by The Italian Table except for the following pages:
33, 45, 51, 63, 75, 81, 87, 93, 99, 105, 117, 129, 135, 141, 147, 153, 165.

Library of Congress Cataloging-in-Publication Data:
Villoresi, Paolo, and Negrin, Micol
Signature Pasta,
by Paolo Villoresi and Micol Negrin

Originally published: New York, The Italian Table, a division of the Italian Culinary Institute, 2000.
Italian Cooking & Living encompasses the multi-media activities (television, internet, video and audio tapes, magazines, and
books) of The Italian Table, a club of Italian food lovers.

ISBN # 0-9705345-0-7

Printed in Italy

First Edition

BOOK DESIGN BY SLAVA PETRAKOV

Technical information:
All food photography was done with the Mamiya RB67 camera,
using 140mm and 90mm lenses. Photos were shot on Fujifilm Provia 100F.

Photograph of Efisio and Francesco Farris on back cover and page 2 by Kennon Evett.

WWW.ITALIANCULINARY.COM

ac**know**ledgments

Putting together a book of this scope requires a lot of effort on the part of dozens of people. We would like to begin by thanking Delverde, for sending us more pasta than we ever thought possible in less time than we had dared to hope, and Urbani, for making sure we had the best bottarga, truffles, porcini, and truffle oil. Thank you to Al Rivera in the fish department at Balducci's, for selecting the finest specimens for our photographs. Our appreciation goes to the following companies, who sent us the plates, glassware, accessories, and linens for our set design: Sferra Bros. Ltd; Bernardaud; Tartufo, Ltd.; Lenox; Pfaltzgraff; Pratesi; Frette; Caleca; Savoir Vivre Int.; Romancing Provence; Casafina; Rosenthal; Commander International Marketing; Williams-Sonoma; Crate & Barrel; Vietri; Cristofle; Emile Henry; and Carole Stupel. We would also like to extend our gratitude to the following companies for providing the wines that appear in the photographs: Opici Import Company; Laird & Company; Bolla Wines; Mionetto; WineWave, Inc.; Empson (U.S.A.) Inc.; and Dufour & Company, Ltd. We extend a thank-you to the folks at Clone-a-Chrome, who treated Jerry Ruotolo's photographs as though they were their own. We are grateful to Livio Panebianco, friend and resident wine expert, for writing an informative chapter on pairing wine with pasta. And, last but certainly not least, our recognition goes to the twenty-six talented chefs who collaborated to make this book a reality we can all be proud of.

contents

pasta and **me**

Paolo Villoresi

Fine Italian Home Made Pasta by Pappo & Dindi Ltd.

I met her when I was a few months old; my mother tells me it took a few years for our friendship to develop, but when I started to ride a tricycle, I grew fond of her, then we became friends and lovers. Our story is long and full of adventures.

When I first moved to the States I landed in Atlanta. Back then, I was married to a lady from the Deep South who thought the city a good compromise between Florence and New York!

With the help of a couple of friends, I soon founded a fresh pasta manufacturing outlet called Pappo & Dindi, Ltd., and I set about getting all the required permits. The first time I went to City Hall, no one there understood just what it was I wanted to do. So I came back a couple of days later, armed with colorful drawings of ravioli and tortellini, but the results were the same: everyone was really nice, but still they didn't know how to help me.

In my new home, I made ravioli, tortellini, and lasagne; I put them in a picnic basket filled with pasta sauces, forks, and napkins, and, carrying a good bottle of wine, I gave it another try. This time, I was successful: everyone at City Hall "knew just how to help me" and encouraged me to return with more of those same delicacies.

That propitious day marked the beginning of a long pasta apprenticeship that has not ended yet. Thirty years ago in Atlanta, the food scene was not what it is today. After setting up my pasta business, I learned that if you wanted to buy good canned Italian plum tomatoes, you had to be Italian, and that a little yelling and cursing was helpful. I also gathered that domestic parmesan cheese was made without a rind, although, if necessary, a thin film of black wax could be applied. The best mozzarella was sold in three-pound squares, ready for the grater, and olive oil was always rancid on the shelves. I learned that people were hungry for innovation, yet baffled when faced with what I was selling. Italian food has come a

long way since the 1970s, not only in Atlanta, but all over America.

I have never stopped discovering new shapes of pasta, new sauces, new and unusual preparation methods. Often, when I read a new recipe for pasta, I have a flash of recognition: the dish, however new, sounds familiar. When I encounter novel pasta interpretations, I taste the food first, then judge it later.

I've met a great deal of chefs, many of whom have demonstrated their recipes in our kitchen at the Italian Culinary Institute. Most often, I've been pleasantly surprised by the quality of the food that they prepare. I've discovered that it's possible to find authentic Italian cuisine in America, thanks to the skilled chefs working in restaurant kitchens and their discerning clientele.

And so the time seemed ripe to publish an altogether different book about pasta, a book that unveils the secrets and the techniques of North America's most talented, creative Italian chefs as they cook Italy's—and now North America's—favorite food. The challenge is to present you with pasta as it exists in this huge, fantastic country today, never losing sight of the traditions from which all the new, enticing ways with pasta have sprung.

Paolo VILLORESI,
New York City

flavors of **home**

"Butto la pasta!" my mother called out nightly from the warmth of our kitchen: "I'm throwing in the pasta!"—a signal clearer than any bell that we should immediately wash our hands and come to the table for our evening meal.

Italians take their pasta seriously. In my family, pasta was a nightly ritual, something we could count on with the same certitude as a daily shower, a kiss before leaving for school or work, a comfortable bed to dream in. It was something we took entirely for granted, like many of the good things we enjoyed every day of our life.

It was when I left home that it hit me. I knew how to cook fairly well by the time I was nineteen, and when I moved out on my own, I experimented wildly in the kitchen. Every night I cooked Thai, Spanish, Chinese, Turkish, something plucked out of a cookbook or a magazine that would transport me to far-away lands. Then, after a few months of stir-fries and kebabs, I felt it: something was missing.

Pasta.

I craved the taste of my childhood, the taste of pasta. I wanted, quite suddenly, to be transported home. From coconut-laced curries and paellas, I turned to more familiar flavors. I asked my mother how she made her shallot sauce, her amatriciana, her pesto, her ragù. I made gnocchi like she had always done, following her proportions exactly, and I sauced them with her Roquefort-curry sauce (a strange but altogether delicious invention of hers). I roasted red peppers and chopped olives, threw them into a pot with diced plum tomatoes and basil, and prepared my favorite sauce of all time for penne.

It took me a long time to make pasta sauces I liked as much as my mother's—pasta sauces that tasted like home—and there are still some I think she makes better than I do. My mother tells me she cooks my roasted fennel sauce for spaghetti three or four times a month now, and makes a leaner pesto with tender basil leaves from her garden in Italy following a recipe I gave her a year ago on the phone. Every week, my mother and I exchange pasta recipes, updating each other on what we have cooked, how it tasted, what we'll try next. Somehow, I know we're trading more than recipes, talking about something much more meaningful than cooking.

With age comes nostalgia, and with nostalgia comes the desire to relive some especially tender moments from the past. I've come to realize that pasta is much more than food for me. It's a way of connecting with my family, a way of experiencing once again the comfort of being a small child—taken care of, well-fed, loved, nourished both physically and emotionally, certain that the next day would dawn benevolent, bringing me just as much joy and pleasure, just as many discoveries, as the day that was quietly closing.

Micol NEGRIN,
New York City

Efisio and Francesco Farris'
malloreddus in wild boar
ragù (recipe on page 96)
is a Sardinian classic.

introduction

Is there a food more symbolic of Italy than pasta? All around the world, people have fallen in love with this classic Italian fare. From shining steel stoves in Japan's top restaurants to country inns in Ireland and home kitchens in Mexico, everyone is cooking pasta and loving it. Long, egg-rich ribbons, short, stout strands, twirled tubes, plump triangles, rustic lozenges—ever since the first bite of pasta was taken by some lucky soul thousands of years ago, the world has been enamored with this simple, nutritious food.

Initially made only from flour and water in its most humble form, pasta has been subsistence food for millennia. But it is so delicious, and so deliciously versatile, that centuries of innovation and ingenuity have given rise to thousands of variations on the basic theme: some pastas are opulent, others rustic, some are boldly flavored, others restrained. There are egg pastas, spinach pastas, squid ink pastas, truffle pastas, herb pastas, pastas made from buckwheat, farro, cornmeal, even rye. There are more pastas than can possibly be eaten in a single lifetime by a devout pasta eater, enough pastas to dazzle the mind and keep any pasta-loving cook busy trying new combinations.

This book was born as a way of celebrating pasta in all its glorious diversity. As the food most symbolic of Italy, pasta has been embraced by chefs across North America, who have put their own stamp—their signature—on Italy's favorite first course. In this volume, we have collected one hundred and twenty-five exciting, vibrant recipes conceived by twenty-six of North America's most creative, renowned chefs.

The pastas that these chefs cook daily in their restaurants are but one link in a long chain of culinary creativity. Just how did the chain get started? When was pasta born, and who made it first? We'll consider these questions and more in this chapter, taking you on a journey of discovery that spans thousands of years and all corners of the globe.

the **origins** of pasta

Almost nowhere is the art and the magic of cooking more apparent, more incredible, than in the birth of pasta. Cooking is a ritual of transformation made possible by divine, purifying fire and by the imagination of the cook, who is in essence an expert manipulator of nature. The transformation from the raw to the cooked is the first magical instance in the cooking process. This metamorphosis becomes an authentic creation when an ingredient is manipulated in such a way that its very essence—its appearance, flavor, and texture—is transformed. And pasta—born of grain and deftly turned into gossamer thin or toothsome sheets of dough which are cut, shaped, twirled, and pinched into an unbelievable number of shapes, then cooked and sauced with an even wider assortment of condiments—pasta is undoubtedly the queen of transformation.

Pasta was likely one of the first foods that humans cooked, one of the first foods to be subjected to the magical, transforming heat of fire. At first the grains were merely crushed between two stones and mixed with water as a sort of porridge, but then someone thought of spreading the porridge on hot stones to cook, giving rise to the first flatbreads and baked pastas of all time. Cooking pasta in this way, on hot stones, is still done in Italy today: in Liguria and Tuscany, for example, testaroli are griddle-baked or roasted over hot stones.

The ancient Greeks certainly enjoyed pasta, as did the Etruscans who inhabited Central Italy three thousand years ago and the ancient Romans who ruled the Mediterranean basin and beyond. The Etruscans even painted funeral frescoes depicting tools used for preparing and cutting pasta, including a wheel for slicing dough that looks strikingly similar to one used today. The Romans ate strips of pasta called laganum, the ancestor of today's lasagna, and they either boiled it, toasted it over hot stones, or fried it—all this a good two thousand years before Marco Polo journeyed to China. Ever fond of delicious

food and the good life, the ancient Romans even made vegetable soups studded with ribbons of pasta. Cicero mentions these pasta and vegetable soups in his writings, and Horace declares that he wants to "go home and sit in front of a good plate of leeks, chickpeas, and laganum."

Until five or six hundred years ago, all manner of pasta, regardless of shape or cut, went by the name maccheroni (or the more ancient maccaroni). Gnocchi, ravioli, fresh, and dried pastas all fell into this category. (Today, maccheroni are a specific type of pasta, short and stout and with a hole in the middle, although many people around the world still refer to all pasta as maccaroni.) Maccheroni were enjoyed both sweet and savory, often doused with honey when they were fried rather than boiled. One recipe dating back to 1500 for maccheroni alla napoletana describes how to fry pasta, then serve it with sugar and honey for a Carnival menu.

Pasta was so central to the Italian diet that the will of a Genoese gentleman named Ponzio Bastone, dated February 2, 1279, even listed one basket of maccheroni among his earthly possessions. Clearly, the maccheroni in question were dried to conserve for long periods of time.

Over the centuries, the types of pasta available multiplied. Vermicelli (from "little worms") became a favored word for pasta, and both fresh and dried pastas were sold under this generic term at the vermicellaio's shop.

dried and stuffed pasta

There is little doubt that the Arabs were the first people to successfully dry pasta (a necessity since they led a largely nomadic life), and that they introduced Sicilians to the art of drying pasta 1,200 years ago. Ibn'al Mibrad, author of the first Arab cookery book, gave instructions for cooking dried pasta back in 700 A.D. Sicily turned out to have the ideal climate for drying pasta, and the practice of drying noodles soon became widespread, moving up to Genoa, Spain, and France, enabling people all over the Mediterranean to conserve one of their staple foods for months.

While most dried pasta was made only of flour and water, using flour milled from whatever grain thrived in a given area, stuffed pasta was less humble. Feast fillings for fresh pasta included fish, seafood, game, and poultry; simpler fillings called only for cheese or vegetables. All these pastas were initially named after medieval savory pies and pastries which contained the same aromatic stuffings.

By 1400, the term ravioli had been born in Genoa, and it referred to two classes of pasta: stuffed pasta that had been cooked in water or broth, then served sprinkled with cheese and spices at the beginning of a meal; and stuffed pasta that had been fried, then drizzled with honey or dusted with sugar and served at the end of a meal.

In 1200, a certain awe-struck Salimbene recounts having eaten "ravioli without dough." These same ravioli are still eaten in Florence today, where they go by the name ravioli ignudi (meaning "naked ravioli", because they are in effect the stuffing for ravioli without the skin). In Emilia-Romagna and Lombardy, the same pasta is called malfatti ("poorly shaped" because of their irregular shape).

For centuries, pasta was classified according to its city of origin: it varied as a result of the grain used, the climate, the water,

Marcelo Gallegos'
fettuccine and figs
(recipe on page 119) is
a novel take on pasta.

the preparation method, the shape, and the sauce paired with it. Pasta in Naples, for instance, was made with a hot water dough; in Liguria, Sicily, and Abruzzo, on the other hand, it was made with cold water.

By the 1600s, Genoa had become a major center for pasta production, leading the Republic of Genoa to control the commerce of wheat all across the Mediterranean and to bring in massive shiploads of wheat from Russia and Canada. In 1749, the town of Savona (about 30 miles from Genoa) became the site of the first commercial pasta manufacturer in Italy.

Naples vied with Genoa for first place as Italy's most important pasta producer. Its factories specialized in long pasta and egg pasta, worked (often by foot!) by men and women as they danced to the beat of the tarantella. Ferdinand II, King of Naples, visited a pasta factory and, seeing the men and women work the dough with their feet, asked one of his engineers to devise a machine for kneading; the new device looked just like two feet, but this time the feet were made of bronze.

Other than Liguria and Campania (or, more succinctly, Genoa and Naples), the two other regions where pasta production developed early were Apulia and Sicily, pushed mostly by the hunger of their people and their swelling population. Pasta was a relatively cheap food with a long shelf life; nourishing, versa-

tile, and easy to cook, it became food for the masses long before it enticed the upper classes. (A great Italian comic actor once said: "People say appetite comes from eating, but I say it comes from not having enough to eat!")

the birth of a national cuisine

Most people think of tomato sauce almost instantly when they think of pasta, even though tomatoes arrived in Italy much later than pasta made its first appearance. A New World import, tomatoes did not top a plate of pasta until the eighteenth century. Until then, pasta was sauced with other vegetables, with meat or fish, with bits of cheese, perhaps even with toasted bread crumbs or a simple drizzle of olive oil. And even when tomatoes did take hold in Italy, it was a while before they became one of the ingredients of choice for saucing pasta, especially in the North.

It was an astute retired banker named Pellegrino Artusi who cleared the path for tomatoes in Northern Italy, and who created a national Italian cuisine by breaking down the culinary boundaries between North and South. The father of modern Italian cuisine, Artusi wrote his highly influential book, "Science in the Kitchen and the Art of Eating Well", in 1891, at a time

when Italy had fallen under the spell of France's cuisine. While Italy had given much to France by way of culinary innovation over the centuries, especially under the reign of the de' Medicis, in the 1700s the tide turned, and Italians began imitating the French style of cooking. Like James Monroe, Artusi—living in Florence, the cultural and culinary capital of Italy at the time—sent out his battle cry: "Italian cuisine for the Italians!" His book was an ode to the values of simple, honest Italian cooking. It presented Italians with the regional specialties of their own country, dishes that few people even knew existed.

Striking a cord in the collective Italian imagination, Artusi's book became a standard in every Italian household. From its hallowed pages, Italians learned to prepare an astounding variety of dishes, including a wonderful array of pastas both fresh and dried: ravioli alla genovese, stuffed with capon, lamb's brain, sweetbreads, and chicken liver; spaghetti with hake and Marsala; pappardelle all'aretina, served in the savory duck sauce typical of Arezzo, Tuscany; and maccheroni con le sarde alla siciliana, a beloved Sicilian dish featuring fresh sardines and anchovies flavored with wild fennel.

pasta for **feasts**

Pasta reigns on Italian tables every day of the year, especially on important celebrations like Carnival and Easter and Christmas. In the North, stuffed pasta is queen: there are the casonsei of Bergamo and Brescia, the squash ravioli of Mantova, the beef-stuffed agnolotti of Piedmont, the meat-stuffed tortellini of Emilia, the cappelletti of Romagna, the ravioli of Tuscany. Emilia is home to the most glorious variations on stuffed

pastas, whereas Southern Italy offers a veritable wealth of dried pasta specialties.

In Verona, home to Romeo and Juliet, Carnival has been dedicated to gnocchi ever since 1400, when a town famine led a wealthy doctor to declare the last Friday of Carnival a day for feasting on gnocchi: A procession is presided over by Papà Gnoc, dressed in a red cloak to symbolize tomato sauce and carrying an oversize fork, and the whole town sits down to enjoy bowls of gnocchi together. In Umbria, handmade squares of pasta are cooked in salted water and topped with sugar, to be served cold as a first course on Christmas. Christmas also brings penne dressed with walnuts, sugar, lemon zest, and cinnamon in Lazio. The Abruzzesi stuff thin, delicate crêpes (Italy's crespelle and Abruzzo's scrippelle) with grated cheese and parsley, then drop them into a bowl of chicken broth for Carnival feasts. In Calabria, short strips of pasta called lagane (very close to the Ancient Romans' beloved laganum) are eaten with beans on Saint Joseph's Day.

Gianni Fassio's scallop and leek conchiglie (recipe on page 101) is a savory marriage of pasta and seafood.

In short, there are hundreds of pasta dishes that are savored across Italy when it's time to celebrate. In fact, if one wanted to eat a different "celebratory" pasta every day, one calendar year wouldn't suffice for a gastronomic tour of Italy.

dried pasta **versus** fresh

Wheat-based pasta is eaten mostly in the Mediterranean, especially in Italy, where over six hundred varieties of it are made. This incredible array of pastas can be classified in many ways. For our purposes, we will consider pasta as forming two categories: fresh pasta, made with soft wheat, semolina, or specialty flours, with or without eggs, for immediate consumption or to be frozen for later use; and dried pasta, produced industrially on a small or large scale with semolina flour (ground from durum wheat) or specialty flours, meant to be conserved for considerable periods of time.

In culinary terms, fresh and dried pasta are two very differ-

ent foods. The first, especially when it is egg-based, is much softer in texture, more delicate. The latter is more rustic, toothsome. And while fresh pasta has an undeniable appeal, especially when it is prepared under our very eyes, dried pasta is better suited to certain dishes. (For more on this, see page 27.)

"Signature Pasta" is dedicated to dried pasta: we give you recipes for saucing and serving nearly every type of dried pasta imaginable, and offer you the tools necessary for cooking it to perfection in your own kitchen. (See page 31.)

But what to make of all the different pasta shapes? Is one really so different from another in terms of taste and texture, or is it just a question of aesthetics? Professor Peter Kubelka, in the introduction to a book entitled "Atlante delle Paste Alimentari", declares that the various pasta shapes can only be "seen" with the mouth. Kubelka also says, rather poetically, that "pasta is architecture for the mouth."

The next time you eat pasta, stop for a moment and consider the range of sensations your mouth is experiencing: the grooves of the pasta on the roof of your mouth, the slipperiness of the pasta, the way its crevices catch bits of sauce and deliver a true flavor punch to your palate. You'll probably agree with Professor Kubelka that only the mouth is able to detect certain differences—almost imperceptible to the naked eye—between one pasta shape and another. These minute variations affect our enjoyment of pasta, mostly as a result of how they interact with the sauce. (For more on this, see page 27.)

the **art** of eating pasta

It may seem strange to consider this now, but until recently, most people ate with their hands. Rich or poor, young or old, men or women: everyone used their hands to scoop and deliver food to the mouth. One thousand years ago, the Doge of Venice married a Byzantine princess who had the sophisticated habit of using a tiny, precious two-pronged fork. Everyone in the princess' circle thought her strange, and considered her fork a diabolical extension of her fingers. When the princess died of the plague, her entourage thought she had incited the wrath of God by her ostentatious display of wealth. Four hundred years later, Catherine de' Medici brought the fork to France, but the fashion still hadn't caught on by the time her son, Henry III, tried to make forks a standard table implement in his court.

And so pasta, like most other foods, was eaten with the hands until a short time ago. In Naples a special technique was devised for carrying "maccheroni" to the mouth with the thumb, the index finger, and the middle finger of the right hand; the noodles were dropped into the waiting mouth as the head tilted back to better receive them. Even King Ferdinand II, who was fond of pasta, was a very skilled eater of maccheroni. His wife, however, was embarrassed by the messy way he ate, so the king ordered one of his engineers to design a four-pronged fork that would allow him to enjoy his cherished pasta without using his hands. Thus the modern fork was born, and along with it the "socially appropriate" way of eating pasta.

If you should happen to try eating pasta with your hands using the old Neapolitan three-finger technique, rather than with a fork, you might just be surprised: yes, you will be uncomfortable, and yes, it will be messy; but the pasta will taste different, and in a strange way, better. Without a fork to mediate between your mouth and the pasta, all you will taste is the pasta itself. Pure, glorious pasta—no more, no less.

how **to use** this book

Before you start cooking the recipes in this book, we suggest that you take a look at our tips for cooking pasta (page 31), which will ensure you a perfect plate of pasta every time you venture into the kitchen. If you feel as strongly as we do that no meal is complete without a good bottle of wine, consult the wine-pairing guide we have included (page 29), which will help you select the appropriate wine for each of your favorite pastas. And to learn which pasta shapes marry best with which sauces, we offer an overview on pairing pasta and sauce (page 27) so that you can experiment fearlessly.

We also provide you with eleven essential sauce recipes (page 17); most are fairly easy to make, and all are worth mastering to widen your pasta repertoire even more. Six of the basic recipes called for throughout the book can be found in a single chapter (page 183), which you can refer to when cooking recipes from other sources as well.

To make identification easier for home cooks, we provide a pasta glossary (page 187) which describes each of the pasta shapes called for in this book. Finally, a list of reputable mail-order sources (page 189) carrying all the ingredients necessary to cook the recipes in this book, and plenty more, is included.

A word of advice: always read the recipe you want to try all the way through before heating a skillet or boiling the water for the pasta. You'll find it much easier to follow the recipe if you are already somewhat familiar with it. We also suggest that you chop, dice, grate, and measure all the necessary ingredients ahead of time, to make cooking more stream-lined.

And now—Buon appetito!

essential sauces
The Italian kitchen offers so many delectable variations on pasta sauces that it is a challenge to synthesize all the knowledge and experimentation and artistry accumulated by imaginative, skilled cooks over three thousand years into a brief little chapter. Just what renders a sauce essential? What makes one version of it—often born of regional preference rather than culinary merit—better than another?

As we pondered this question, we realized that a sauce becomes a culinary essential when it liberates the cook, when it opens new doors, when it reflects a general tendency in a nation's cuisine, or when—quite simply—it is too good to pass up. Some of the essential sauces every cook should have in his or her arsenal are already featured in the book as part of the chefs' signature recipes; others, too good not to be shared, we give you here.

There are eleven main categories of sauces for pasta: each category refers to the main ingredient in the sauce, the ingredient that defines the flavor and texture and character of the sauce. They are: tomato sauces; herb sauces; olive oil-based sauces; egg-based sauces; cream sauces; fish and seafood sauces; meat sauces; legume sauces; cheese sauces; bread crumb sauces; and nut sauces.

tomato sauces

Tomato sauce and pasta go hand in hand, so much so that it's nearly impossible for some people to imagine cooking pasta and not tossing it with a tomato-based sauce. But in reality, tomatoes were not widely used in the Italian kitchen until roughly 1700: they had arrived from Chile after Columbus returned from America, but most Europeans were wary of them, believing them to be poisonous. Tomatoes were grown as ornamental plants rather than food for a long time after they reached European shores, and it took centuries before cooks began to use the versatile fruit. Today, the average Italian eats 110 pounds of tomatoes a year, and quite a bit of these are cooked into sauce for pasta, especially in the South of Italy.

In the beginning of the nineteenth century, Naples became the world capital of pummarola'n coppa, tomato sauce meant for topping the city's famous pasta, and the Neapolitans remain unabashedly fond of tomatoes to this day. Italian immigrants who came to North America in the early 1900s brought recipes for their beloved tomato sauce with them, and so the love affair with tomatoes came full circle, as a New World food was returned to the New World in an entirely novel guise by Old World cooks.

It's impossible to tell you which tomato sauce, among the thousands of tomato sauces that exist, is best: one featuring only garlic and basil (see page 185)? One studded with an aromatic medley of carrots, celery, and onions, as most restaurant chefs prepare in their kitchens? One using minced scallions only, tossed into sizzling olive oil for flavor? One that calls for fresh tomatoes rather than canned?

Here we bow to Pellegrino Artusi, gastronome, father of modern Italian cuisine, and author of "Science in the Kitchen and the Art of Eating Well" (see page 13 for more on Artusi), and offer you his classic, all-purpose recipe for tomato sauce.

artusi's tomato sauce
- 8 ripe plum tomatoes
- $1/4$ onion, minced
- 1 garlic clove, minced
- $1/4$ celery stalk, minced
- 6 basil leaves, torn
- 6 Italian parsley sprigs, minced
- $1/3$ cup extra-virgin olive oil
- $1/4$ teaspoon salt

Bring 4 quarts of water to a boil. Make a cross on the bottom of each tomato and drop into the water; cook 1 minute. Remove with a slotted spoon to a bowl filled with cold water. Slip the peels off the tomatoes, cut off the stem end, and cut in half. Scoop out the seeds and dice with a sharp knife.

Cook the onion, garlic, celery, basil, and parsley in the olive oil until all the vegetables are soft and the onion is translucent, about 10 minutes over medium-low heat. Add the tomatoes and salt; bring to a gentle boil and simmer, covered, until the sauce is thick and aromatic, about 30 minutes. Taste for salt, adding some if needed, and serve hot. Makes about 2 cups

Variation: Artusi suggests straining the sauce.

herb sauces

The Italian kitchen relies on a plethora of fragrant herbs for flavor: basil, sage, rosemary, parsley (the flat-leaf variety, never the curly), mint, chives, oregano, savory, marjoram, chervil, and dill are the most frequent herbs called for in Italian cooking. Herbs are minced, then added to the aromatic vegetables in a pasta sauce, where they lend an underlying flavor to the sauce.

But they also star in pasta sauces all on their own: the most obvious example is basil pesto, a simple sauce that Genoese cooks have perfected and made famous all around the world (see page 43 for a recipe). There are countless variations on pesto, a word that is derived from the verb pestare, meaning 'to pound', because the herbs are usually pounded to a paste in a mortar with a pestle. There is the parsley pesto of Sicily, which includes almonds for a subtle, nutty flavor; the basil and walnut pesto of Tuscany; and numerous pestos created spontaneously in Italian kitchens across the globe to make the most of fragrant, just-plucked garden herbs. All pestos, of course, call for olive oil, which is slowly poured in until the mixture emulsifies and which gives the sauce its rich texture.

Here we offer you an unusual pesto made with arugula, basil, and olives; it lends itself beautifully to short pastas and gnocchi alike. (For other pestos, see pages 59, 139, and 144.)

arugula-basil pesto

   3 bunches arugula, washed, stems removed
   2 cups packed tender basil leaves
   2 garlic cloves, peeled
   $^1/_4$ teaspoon chili flakes
   $^1/_2$ cup black oil-cured olives, pitted
   1 cup extra-virgin olive oil, plus extra if needed
   1 cup freshly grated Parmigiano Reggiano
   salt

Bring 2 quarts of water to a boil and drop in the arugula leaves. Cook for 1 minute, or until the leaves wilt; drain, drop into a bowl of cold water to stop the cooking and set the color, and cool. Drain, then squeeze dry to remove every last bit of moisture from the leaves (this is very important, because if the arugula is moist it will make for a watery pesto).

Place the arugula, basil, garlic, chili, and olives in the bowl of a food processor; pulse to blend until nearly smooth. Begin adding the olive oil in a thin, steady stream while the motor is running; the mixture will emulsify. Add more olive oil if needed to obtain a thick, creamy sauce. Turn out into a bowl, fold in the Parmigiano with a rubber spatula, and season with salt.

Refrigerate for up to 2 days, covered with a thin film of olive oil to prevent the sauce from turning black.

When you are ready to serve the pasta, dilute the pesto with ¼ cup of the pasta cooking water before folding in the cooked pasta. Makes about 2 cups

olive oil-based sauces

Olive oil has become the cooking fat of choice all across Italy, as health concerns have caused butter-loving Northern Italians and those fond of lard to adopt this golden liquid for all manner of cooking. So it's not surprising that most sauces for pasta are, in fact, olive oil-based. Before tomatoes arrived in Europe, and in most country kitchens, pasta was typically tossed only with a few drops of olive oil, perhaps dusted with a touch of cheese or a sprinkle of herbs or spices for additional flavor.

One sauce stands out as the most elementary and satisfying among all the olive oil-based sauces for pastas: aglio, olio e peperoncino is one of Italy's favorite condiments for pasta, especially spaghetti. After all, could there be anything more satisfying on a tired winter night than a plate of pasta tossed with a bracing, chili- and garlic-laced olive oil sauce? This sauce is peasant cuisine at its most ingenious: two intensely aromatic, easy-to-come-by, inexpensive ingredients mingle with olive oil to create a true taste explosion. (For a recipe, see page 100.)

Other excellent olive oil-based sauces call for melting anchovies with minced garlic and a touch of chili in olive oil, or tossing minced Italian parsley or other herbs into warmed olive oil. Among the best olive oil-based sauces is Lazio's olio, cacio e pepe sauce for spaghetti. Here is the recipe.

olive oil, cracked pepper, and pecorino sauce
    ½ cup extra-virgin olive oil
    ½ cup freshly grated Pecorino Romano
    1 teaspoon cracked black pepper

Combine the olive oil, Pecorino, and cracked black pepper in a bowl large enough to accommodate 1 pound of cooked spaghetti. When you drain the spaghetti, reserve ⅓ cup of the pasta cooking water, and add it to the bowl along with the spaghetti, then toss and serve immediately. Makes about 1 cup

egg-based sauces

Comfort food at its best: pasta tossed with a velvety sauce, perhaps accented by a little cracked black pepper or some browned pancetta cubes. This is carbonara: a creamy sauce created in a mere minute by beating eggs with grated, fragrant Parmigiano, it is one of Italy's quintessential sauces and one of Rome's most famous offerings. (See page 61 for a recipe.)

Other examples of egg-based sauces abound in Italy, especially in the countryside, where a few good ingredients have ritually been turned into delectable feasts by smart cooks. One of the most succulent egg sauces for pasta is prepared in Campania and paired with short pasta tubes like tubetti.

creamy egg and parmigiano sauce
    3 eggs
    ½ cup freshly grated Parmigiano Reggiano
    5 tablespoons unsalted butter
    1 tablespoon minced Italian parsley

Beat the eggs with the Parmigiano in a small bowl. When you are ready to serve, melt the butter in a skillet large enough to accommodate 1 pound of short pasta. Toss in the drained pasta, and quickly fold in the egg-Parmigiano mixture, stirring for 1 minute over high heat to coat the pasta and thicken the egg. Serve hot, topped with the parsley. Makes about 1 cup

cream sauces

Despite the star billing that cream-based pasta sauces have received on restaurant menus both in Italy and in North America lately, only a handful of traditional Italian pasta sauces call for significant amounts of heavy cream. While a touch of cream is often poured into the skillet where a sauce happily bubbles away, lending it a luscious mouthfeel and delicate flavor, cream sauces are the exception to the rule in the Italian kitchen. There are times, however, when nothing else will do, times when the decadence of a creamy plate of pasta is just what you need to restore your spirit and please your palate.

So for those moments, we offer you a subtle, saffron-laced cream sauce from Emilia. The peas can be omitted if you prefer, but they add a lovely green color that contrasts beautifully with the gold of the saffron.

saffron-laced cream sauce
  1 onion, minced
  4 tablespoons unsalted butter
  8 ounces frozen or shelled fresh peas
  4 ounces Prosciutto Cotto, diced
  1 1/2 cups heavy cream
  1/2 teaspoon saffron
  salt and freshly ground black pepper
  1 cup freshly grated Parmigiano Reggiano

In a skillet large enough to hold 1 pound of pasta, sauté the onion in the butter until golden and soft, about 10 minutes over medium-low heat. Add the peas and cook 2 more minutes. Fold in the Prosciutto, and cook 1 minute. Pour in the cream; bring to a boil. Add the saffron and stir to dissolve. Season with salt and pepper, fold in the Parmigiano, and cook 1 more minute.

When you are ready to serve, toss 1 pound of cooked pasta (tagliatelle and garganelli are best) with the sauce in the skillet for 30 seconds to mingle the flavors. Serve hot, dusted with additional Parmigiano. Makes about 2 cups

fish and seafood sauces

If you've ever been to a fish market in Italy, you know that Italians love their fish and seafood. There are so many creatures swimming in the Mediterranean—many of which don't even exist here—that a cook could literally prepare a different fish or seafood sauce every night. Tiny octopus are stewed to supple perfection in heady tomato sauces flavored with basil and oregano; cubes of monkfish are simmered with saffron and cream until meltingly tender; succulent baby clams are bathed in wine until they open to reveal their pearly interiors; gorgeous, pastel-hued scampi are tossed into sizzling pans with chili, parsley, and garlic; scorpionfish and other creatures of the sea are turned into savory sauces accented by celery, wine, and tomatoes; lobster, shrimp, mussels, and scallops mingle in aro-

matic sauces that please the eye as much the palate.

Some sauces are velvety, others chunky. Some call for a combination of fish and seafood for more intense flavor (these were often born in fishmongers' kitchens as a way of using up whatever fish could not be sold at market on any given day and have become hallowed classics over the years); others use only one variety of fish or shellfish. The most beloved sauce in this category is probably clam sauce, which can be cooked with or without tomato sauce. (See page 68 for a recipe.)

Among all the variations on fish sauces, one stands out as a good, basic sauce that tastes simply of fish: made across Liguria, it uses an assortment of fish for intensity and depth. Remember that the uglier the fish, the better the flavor, so don't steer clear of homely specimens like monkfish and scorpionfish.

simple genoese fish sauce

    2 pounds assorted fish, heads on (scorpionfish, red mullet,
        monkfish, and turbot are ideal)
    $^{1}/_{2}$ cup extra-virgin olive oil
    1 onion, thinly sliced
    1 rosemary sprig
    1 tablespoon minced Italian parsley
    salt

Rinse the fish and place it in a wide pan. Add just enough water to cover, bring to a gentle boil over medium heat, and cook for 2 minutes. Remove the fish from the pan with a slotted spoon, reserving the cooking water, and remove the skin and bones; coarsely chop the fish.

Heat the olive oil in a saucepan and add the minced fish. Cook for 5 minutes, or until golden all over, then add the onion,

rosemary, parsley, and the reserved cooking water, and bring to a gentle boil. Season with salt, and simmer for 30 minutes. Pass through a food mill fitted with a medium disk, discard the solids, and pour the sauce into a clean saucepan. Bring to a gentle boil and simmer for 15 minutes, or until thick and reduced. Adjust the salt if needed.

When you are ready to serve, cook $1^{1}/_{2}$ pounds of pasta (preferably trenette or mafaldine) until al dente, then drain and toss with the sauce, adding some of the pasta cooking water if needed to dilute the consistency. Makes about 3 cups

Variation: You can add 1 pound of diced plum tomatoes along with the onion, rosemary, and parsley for a red sauce. Other versions call for leaving the fish in chunks rather than passing it through a food mill.

meat sauces

Romagna, Abruzzo, Sardinia, Campania, Apulia: All these regions make one form of ragù or another. Ragù—a term that comes from the French word ragoût—describes a meat-based sauce most often paired with pasta. Italian ragùs fall into two distinct groups: those made with finely ground or knife-minced meat, and those made by slowly braising an entire cut of meat in sauce until fork-tender.

Ragù is featured on most feast tables across Italy, tossed with stuffed or dried pasta as a symbol of abundance and celebration. There are pork ragùs in and around Naples, lamb ragùs in Romagna, beef ragùs in Lombardy, three-meat ragùs in Emilia. Of course, the most famous ragù of all is the one made in Bologna: ragù alla bolognese, as perfect with lasagna as it is lovely with tagliatelle or garganelli. Here is our favorite recipe for it.

ragù alla bolognese

- 3 tablespoons unsalted butter
- 3 ounces pancetta, diced
- 1 onion, minced
- 1 celery stalk, minced
- 1 carrot, minced
- 4 ounces ground pork
- 4 ounces ground beef
- 1 cup dry red wine
- 2 cups beef broth, heated
- 1 teaspoon tomato paste
- salt and freshly ground black pepper
- 8 ounces plum tomatoes, peeled, seeded, and diced

Melt the butter in a large pot and add the pancetta, onion, celery, and carrot; cook for about 15 minutes, stirring often, over medium heat; the vegetables and pancetta should not color.

Add the ground pork and beef, and cook until lightly browned all over, stirring often; it should take about 15 minutes. Pour in $^1/_2$ cup of the wine, reduce the liquid by half, and add $^1/_2$ cup of the heated broth. Cook until all the liquid in the pot has been absorbed, then pour in another $^1/_2$ cup of the broth, the tomato paste, and the remaining wine. Cook until the liquid in the pot has been absorbed, pour in $^1/_2$ cup more of the broth, season with salt and pepper, and fold in the tomatoes. Cover; simmer until the ragù thickens, about 30 minutes; pour in the remaining broth, cover, and cook for 1 more hour. Adjust the salt if needed, and keep warm.

When you are ready to serve, cook 1 pound of egg pasta (tagliatelle or garganelli are best) and drain; toss with the ragù, adding a tablespoon or two of unsalted butter if you like, and serve hot. Makes about 3 cups

legume sauces

As long as 2,500 years ago, the ancient Romans were relishing pasta tossed with vegetables and legumes. To this day, Italians marry lentils, chickpeas, cranberry beans, cannellini beans, and black-eyed peas with pasta—not only in pasta e fagioli, which finds multiple interpretations across Italy, but in simple first courses that are both nourishing and quick to put together.

Romans love their pasta with lentils, Neapolitans their pasta with cannellini beans, Emilians their pasta with cranberry beans. All are delicious. The following chickpea sauce for pasta, usually served with short strips of pasta called lagane in Southern Italy (Apulia, Calabria, and Basilicata), can serve as a model for all legume-based pasta sauces, being exactly halfway between creamy and chunky. Of course, it is best made with dried chickpeas, but we offer you an easier version using canned chickpeas so that you can make it on short notice, when the craving strikes or the doorbell rings, bringing unannounced guests.

chickpea sauce

- one 15-ounce can chickpeas, drained and rinsed
- $^1/_2$ cup extra-virgin olive oil
- 1 dried chili pepper, crumbled
- 2 garlic cloves, chopped
- 1 onion, minced
- 1 tablespoon minced Italian parsley
- 12 basil leaves, torn

1 bay leaf
3 tomatoes, peeled, seeded, and chopped
salt and freshly ground black pepper

Place all but $1/4$ cup of the chickpeas in a food processor; add 1 cup of water and process until smooth.

Heat the olive oil with the chili and garlic in a 1-quart saucepan. Add the onion, parsley, basil, and bay leaf; cook, stirring, about 5 minutes over medium heat. Add the whole chickpeas, puréed chickpeas, tomatoes, salt, and pepper; bring to a boil and simmer, covered, for 30 minutes, stirring every 10 minutes. You may need to add a little water as the sauce cooks if the liquid reduces too much. Discard the bay leaf.

When you are ready to serve, transfer the hot chickpea sauce to a heated bowl large enough to accommodate 1 pound of cooked pappardelle or lasagne. Dilute with $1/4$ cup of the pasta cooking water, and fold in the pasta. It is customary to serve the pasta drizzled with olive oil, dusted with freshly grated Pecorino Romano, and sprinkled with freshly ground black pepper. Makes about 2 cups

cheese sauces

Gorgonzola, Grana Padano, Parmigiano, Ricotta, Fontina, Caciotta, Scamorza, Mozzarella, Crescenza, Provolone, Taleggio, Robiola, Pecorino: the list goes on and on. Visit any cheese shop and you'll be amazed at the variety of firm, soft, blue-veined, creamy, and spreadable cheeses that Italy produces. Some are best grated over pasta, the final flourish that pulls all other flavors in the dish together. (See page 24 for a word on grating cheeses for pasta.) Others are especially suitable for cooking, and lend themselves beautifully to pasta sauces.

The most renowned example of a melted cheese sauce is Italy's sumptuous quattro formaggi, featuring four cheeses. (See page 42 for a recipe.) Another classic example is Fontina-laced fonduta. (See page 104 for a recipe.) But a little-known gem is Lazio's fresh ricotta sauce for spaghetti and maccheroni, which we offer you here. A touch sweet, it is commonly served for feasts and celebrations; in Italy, it is usually made with sheep's milk ricotta, which can be found in some specialty shops across North America (see page 189 for sources).

cinnamon-scented ricotta sauce

5 ounces fresh ricotta, preferably sheep's milk
$1/2$ cup whole milk
1 tablespoon sugar
$1/10$ teaspoon freshly ground cinnamon

Place the ricotta in a sieve set over a bowl, and push it through using a rubber spatula; this step helps to eliminate any lumps from the ricotta. Using a wire whisk, beat in the milk, then add the sugar and cinnamon. Turn out into a bowl that is large enough to hold 1 pound of cooked pasta.

When you drain the pasta, reserve $1/3$ cup of the pasta cooking water and fold it into the sauce along with the pasta. Makes about 1 cup

In Italy, when people refer to perfect pairings, they say "come il cacio sui maccheroni:" like cheese on pasta. There are hundreds of Italian cheeses, some of which have found their way to

America and some of which have not. Many are used for cooking, as well as for eating at the table, while others are more frequently called upon as grating cheeses. The most common grating cheeses are Parmigiano Reggiano, Grana Padano, Pecorino (usually Romano, but also Toscano or Sardo or Siciliano), and Ricotta Salata.

Not all pastas call for a sprinkling of grated cheese (those with fish and seafood, or those with garlic and anchovy, often do not), but when cheese is called for, the one you choose will make a difference in the final character of the dish. Parmigiano and Grana are warm, nutty in flavor, best suited to creamy sauces and subtle tomato or meat sauces; Ricotta Salata, being a salted ricotta, suits sharp, pungent vegetable sauces, especially tomato sauces with olives, chili, or capers; and Pecorino is ideal with tomato sauces featuring pork, pancetta, bacon, lamb, or other intensely savory ingredients, and with creamy, egg-based sauces that contrast beautifully with its sharp flavor.

Each of the recipes in this book suggests the most appropriate cheese for a given pasta, but you should feel free to explore, to try out other cheeses just to see how the flavors of the dish change. After all, cooking is equal parts art and magic, tradition and inspiration.

bread crumb sauces

Bread crumbs (mollica in Italian, muddica in dialect) have long served as thickeners in sauces in place of more costly nuts, cream, or cheese, and have been a favored topping for pasta for the same reason, replacing these costlier ingredients and turning stale bread into a condiment. Southern Italians are especially fond of sprinkling toasted bread crumbs over a finished pasta dish, and of folding bread crumbs into olive oil-based pasta sauces for body and flavor: why waste stale bread, after all, when you can transform it into savory crumbs?

One tip: If you have leftover bread, process it into crumbs by grinding it in a food processor until fine but not powdery—and avoid the flavored bread crumbs available on the market, which are often rancid and taste like old garlic rather than good, wheaty bread.

Cooks in Calabria, Sicily, Basilicata, Sardinia, and Apulia have a great repertoire of pasta sauces that incorporate bread crumbs. One of the best examples is from Sicily, and calls for anchovies, garlic, parsley, chili flakes, and olive oil as a flavor base.

bread crumb-anchovy sauce from siracusa
$1/2$ cup extra-virgin olive oil
2 garlic cloves, crushed
8 salted anchovies, gutted, boned, and rinsed
1 dried chili pepper, crumbled
2 tablespoons minced Italian parsley
$2/3$ cup fresh bread crumbs

Heat all but 1 tablespoon of the olive oil in a skillet. Add the garlic, and cook until aromatic, about 30 seconds over medium heat; discard the garlic.

Add the anchovies to the olive oil in the skillet and cook, crushing with a fork to break them down, until they dissolve, about 2 minutes; stir in the chili and parsley, and cook for 30 more seconds. Remove from the heat.

Meanwhile, in a second skillet, heat the remaining olive oil.

Add the bread crumbs and cook until golden all over and toasted, about 2 minutes over medium heat, stirring often. Remove from the heat.

When you are ready to serve, place the warm anchovy-olive oil sauce in a serving bowl large enough to hold 1 pound of cooked bucatini or spaghetti. Add the pasta, along with $1/4$ cup of the pasta cooking water, and toss; adjust the seasoning, and serve hot, sprinkled with the toasted bread crumbs. Makes about $1\,1/2$ cups

nut sauces

The Amalfi Coast is home to the best walnuts in Italy, Sicily to the best almonds, Liguria to the best pine nuts, Piedmont to the best hazelnuts: every region has a favored nut and a wealth of pasta sauces featuring nuts. Nut sauces can be cold or hot, creamy or chunky, olive oil-based or cream-based. They can be used to coat short or long pasta, gnocchi, and all manner of stuffed pasta. But no matter what corner of Italy a nut sauce hails from, you can be sure of one thing: in each and every recipe, the nut remains the star in the sauce. Other ingredients play a supporting role, serving only to bring out the nut's own distinct flavor: if there is garlic, it will not be overwhelming; if there is chili, it's bound to be a mere pinch or two; if there are fresh herbs, they will underscore the nut's characteristic taste rather than mask it.

One of the greatest nut sauces Italy offers is a walnut creation from Liguria, a heady combination of walnuts, pine nuts, olive oil, and garlic that marries splendidly with the region's cheese- and wild greens-stuffed pasta, plump little ravioli called pansotti. The recipe below utilizes cream as a thickener; older recipes suggest bread instead, which is much less expensive and yields a lighter sauce.

Whichever nut sauce you choose to make, be sure that the nuts you use are fresh: nuts have quite a high fat content, and go rancid very quickly. To ensure the nuts you buy are fresh, shop at a store with a good turnover of merchandise, and refrigerate nuts when you bring them home from the market.

ligurian walnut sauce
$1\,1/2$ cups shelled walnut halves
$1/2$ cup pine nuts
1 garlic clove, peeled
$1/16$ teaspoon freshly grated nutmeg (optional)
salt and freshly ground black pepper
$1/2$ cup freshly grated Parmigiano Reggiano
1 cup extra-virgin olive oil, plus extra if needed
$1/2$ cup heavy cream

Combine all the ingredients except the olive oil and cream in a food processor. Purée until creamy. With the motor running, add the olive oil in a thin, steady stream, then work in the cream; the mixture should be fluid yet dense. Add more olive oil if needed to thin out the sauce.

When you are ready to serve, place the walnut sauce in a heated serving bowl large enough to hold 1 pound of cooked penne or other pasta (a special type of greens-stuffed ravioli are the pasta of choice in Liguria, but dried short pasta is lovely too). Stir in $1/3$ cup of the pasta cooking water, then fold in the pasta and serve hot. Makes about 2 cups

Roberto Bernardoni's bucatini in rich tomato-pancetta sauce (recipe on page 53) is a perfect example of pairing pasta and sauce.

pairing pasta & sauce
Long, short, ridged, smooth, flavored with egg or squid ink or spinach—pasta comes in an incredible variety of shapes and textures, sizes and flavors. Not surprisingly, these diverse pastas are best savored with different sauces...

Just how to pair pasta with its most appropriate sauce is one thing that most Italian cooks agree on. Considering that Italians have been making pasta for thousands of years, it isn't surprising that there are strong traditions when it comes to matching a specific pasta with a specific sauce: certain pasta shapes are indigenous to certain geographic areas, and in those very areas, there are certain foods that people eat more often than not. As a result, the coupling of regional pastas with regional sauces makes perfect sense. Take, for instance, trofie: these short, twirled gnocchi from the Italian Riviera are almost always paired with basil pesto. Why? Because the birthplace of trofie is also home to Italy's most fragrant basil pesto. Pesto not only has the right consistency for coating the slightly floury, rustic trofie—it is also a favorite condiment among the people who make trofie in the first place. There are countless other examples of this type: bucatini paired with amatriciana sauce, egg tagliatelle in cream sauces, zite with meatballs. Each of these pairings speaks of a long regional culinary tradition, and tastes wonderful to boot.

But while what custom dictates is often right, it isn't the only basis on which you can pair pastas and sauces. You can certainly follow your instincts and try out pairings that you think would work. A few tips might be helpful as you explore the universe of dried pasta and ponder which sauce to marry with your favorite pasta shape.

Consider all the various shapes of dried pasta available on the market as belonging to seven distinct categories, each of which is best suited to specific sorts of sauces. The categories are based on factors that influence how effectively the pasta will grab onto sauce: texture (ridged versus smooth); length

(short versus long); hollowness (with a hole in the middle or without); flavoring ingredients (egg, spinach, squid ink, tomato, saffron, etc...); and diameter. Armed with the brief pairing scheme below, you'll have no trouble at all finding the perfect mate for your pasta of choice.

short smooth pasta This group includes penne, sedani, ditali, mezze zite, and so on. It is best paired with fairly smooth, cream or tomato-based sauces, because the pasta's slippery texture makes holding onto chunks more difficult. If the pasta has large holes, however (conchiglie, for instance), it is also appropriate with chunky sauces, since the pieces can find a comfortable home in the pasta's cavities.

short ridged pasta Penne rigate, rigatoni, fusilli rigati, and other short ridged pastas are ideal with meat sauces, chunky vegetable sauces, and sauces that contain large elements like shrimp or meatballs, which can nestle in the holes of the pasta. The ridges grab onto the sauce better, so the sauce need not be smooth to bind easily.

long pasta without a hole The tendency is to marry cream-based sauces with flat pastas (linguine, tagliatelle), especially if they are egg-based, rather than with cylindrical pastas (spaghetti, capellini). Great with tomato-based meat or vegetable sauces.

long pasta with a hole Bucatini, zite, and other long pastas with a hole are even better than long, cylindrical pastas without a hole (such as spaghetti) for grabbing onto chunky ingredients. Cream sauces with meat or seafood are also good choices.

egg pasta There are a number of dried pastas made with egg. Both long (tagliatelle, fettuccine) and short ones (garganelli) are best with cream sauces, because of the delicate taste the egg confers to the pasta. Meat sauces are also excellent partners.

flavored pasta This group contains diverse pastas, so a list of pairings is impossible. Sauces that marry with whole wheat pasta don't necessary marry with squid ink pasta, for example, so you have to let your mental palate be your guide.

tiny pasta This category is usually reserved for soup. It includes acini di pepe, orzo (which can, however, be used to make a good risotto-like pasta as well), stelline, quadratini, and other pastas with a very small diameter. Use larger pastas for chunkier soups, like minestrone, and smaller pastas for liquid soups, like chicken noodle soup.

pairing pasta & wine

In Italy, there is no such thing as a good meal without a good bottle of wine. Whether you are cooking a simple pasta or an elaborate one, your enjoyment of the dish will surely be heightened by pouring the perfect wine alongside.

Franco Barone's sicilian timballo (recipe on page 47) is rich enough to pair with a medium-bodied red wine.

Pasta and wine are both deeply rooted in the Italian gastronomic tradition, and so it seems only logical that the pairing of wine with pasta deserves a great deal of attention. Unfortunately, the prevailing philosophy—both in the professional wine world, and in the world of food at large—is that an appropriate pairing of pasta and wine is either of little consequence, or impossible to achieve. Why, if it is so important to match wine with fish, seafood, meat, poultry, cheeses, and even desserts, should mating pasta with its most ideal wine be incidental? And why should it seem so daunting a task for those who would like to try their hand at it? In this brief little chapter, I'd like to offer you the parameters that guide me as I select the best wine to pour with any given pasta.

Rather than looking at the type of pasta being served—long, short, ridged, or smooth—the most important factor, and the only one you really need to pay attention to, is the sauce. In other words, put the accent on the seasoning, not the noodle. To achieve a harmonious combination of pasta and wine, consider which wine would marry better with the sauce at hand. Remember, however, that pasta has a thinning effect on the flavors of the sauce. For example, if we would happily pair a rich game dish with a full-bodied, tannic wine like Barolo or Brunello di Montalcino, we should think twice before serving the same wine with a dish of pappardelle in game ragù: the intensity of the game is toned down by the bulk and the neutral taste of the pasta, so that we would in effect be better off with a well-structured but less full-bodied wine, like Barbaresco or Chianti Classico Riserva. This concept applies to all pasta sauces: whichever wine you would pour alongside a given dish, choose a wine that is one notch less intense when those same ingredients are presented in a pasta sauce.

As I just pointed out, pastas in game sauces are best savored with sufficiently well-structured wines like Barbaresco, Chianti Classico Riserva, Amarone, and Aglianico del Vulture.

Pastas in lighter meat sauces—a basic beef ragù, for instance—pair wonderfully with medium-bodied, fruity wines of low acidity like Freisa, Rosso di Montepulciano, or Valpolicella Classico. Here you're looking for a wine with low acid-

ity to contrast with the acidity of the tomato that is likely cooked into the ragù.

Pastas with white meat (veal or chicken, and to a certain extent pork) are better enjoyed with both whites or medium-bodied reds. Try Pinot Grigio and Sauvignon for a white, or a Dolcetto, Barbera d'Alba, or Tuscan Sangiovese for a red.

With fish-based sauces, or sauces that include seafood (like spaghetti with red mullet, linguine with mussels, or capellini with scampi), turn to fresh, dry white wines that are delicately aromatic. The alcohol content of the following wines is perfect for fish and seafood pastas: Gavi, Vermentino Ligure, Fiano di Avellino, Vernaccia di San Gimignano, and Ribolla Gialla.

Tomato-based sauces marry well with whites or reds. I tend to like Soave Classico, Lugana, and Verdicchio; for reds, I often choose a Chianti Classico or a Barbera d'Alba aged in barrique (the barrique aging softens the acidity of the wine).

Cream-based sauces call for lightly aromatic whites like Cinque Terre, Vernaccia di San Gimignano, or Traminer, which nicely counter the richness of the cream.

Artichokes are notoriously tough for wine pairing, because of their high iron content. With artichoke-based sauces, you should opt for a wine that contrasts with the artichoke's strong flavor without being overwhelmed by it: Nebbiolo or Refosco are good as far as reds go, and Gavi di Gavi is a white I would heartily recommend.

Sauces that feature mushrooms require special attention. As a result of the mushrooms' heady fragrance, dishes featuring mushrooms should not be paired with highly tannic or acidic wines. Opt for a rosé: Bardolino Chiaretto, Lagrein Kretzer, Chiaretto del Garda, or Rosato del Salento are wonderful.

Pasta dishes that include vegetables with slightly bitter tendencies (radicchio and eggplants, for instance) are best accompanied by soft whites with a low acidity level; because of the vegetables' own potent bouquet, pour a wine that is not very aromatic. Ideal wines include Inzolia di Sicilia, Vermentino di Gallura, Alcamo Bianco, Ravello Bianco, and Locorotondo.

On the other hand, legume-based pasta sauces (which run the gamut from a good old-fashioned bowl of pasta e fagioli to a lentil or chickpea sauce for penne or garganelli) call for young, fresh reds like Chianti, Dolcetto, Merlot del Veneto, and Rossese di Dolceacqua.

Finally, a word about which wines are best suited for use in the pasta pot, rather than alongside the pasta bowl. In other words, which wine should you be reaching for when a recipe instructs you to "deglaze the pan with the wine?" Here I would suggest that you use the same wine for cooking as you would for drinking with a given pasta.

One word of caution before you open a bottle of Sassicaia to deglaze your pheasant ragù: avoid using very expensive, truly glorious wines for cooking. Wine's unique organoleptic characteristics are altered during the cooking process—its sugars intensify, acidity decreases, and so on—so you won't really taste a wine's singular character once the sauce has finished cooking. Don't waste a truly wonderful wine in the pasta sauce. Savor it alongside instead—and rejoice in one of the most profoundly gratifying, and absolutely Italian, food pairings of all time: a perfect glass of wine with a perfect plate of pasta.

Livio PANEBIANCO,
President and Founder, Panebianco Imports,
New York City

pasta cooking tips Preparing a perfect

plate of pasta is not complicated, but it does require that you follow a few basic techniques. And while all the chefs in this book will each have their own tricks and secrets when it comes to making pasta sauces, rest assured that they all agree on the appropriate method of cooking the pasta.

Start with good quality pasta: there are a number of excellent pasta brands, and some chefs swear by one rather than another. All chefs, however, will tell you that they use only imported Italian pasta: it has the right humidity content and toothiness to ensure an al dente texture (more on that later).

Next is the water. Water is the cooking medium of choice for pasta, unless you are serving pasta in soup (broth is the liquid of choice in this case). The rule is 1 quart of boiling water for every 3½ ounces (100 grams) of pasta, whether you are making short or long pasta. More water is fine, but less is not: the pasta will stick and cook unevenly in a small quantity of water.

Salt is also important. When the water comes to a boil, and only then, add 10 to 12 grams of salt per quart of water (2 teaspoons to 2½ teaspoons); adding salt before the water comes to a boil makes the water come to a boil more slowly, something to consider when you are trying to get dinner on the table quickly. (Some chefs will tell you that if you let the salted water boil a while, the water will end up tasting metallic.)

Stirring is another crucial step. When you add the pasta to the boiling water, stir vigorously; if you are making long pasta, keep stirring with a long-handled fork or spoon until the pasta loses its rigidity and is entirely submerged in the water. Stir every 30 seconds or so as the pasta cooks. Adding oil to the water is unnecessary: it will reduce sticking, but the oily coating will also prevent the sauce from grabbing onto the pasta.

Keeping the water at a steady boil ensures even cooking: to do so, put the lid on the pot as soon as you have stirred the pasta into the water, and remove it only long enough to stir. If the water is not maintained at a rapid boil, the pasta will cook through faster on the outside and remain raw on the inside.

Regardless of what the package instructions tell you about cooking time, start tasting pasta fairly early to check how it's coming along, and taste it every 15 seconds as it gets closer to being done. Pasta should always be al dente ("to the tooth"), a reference to the infinitesimal resistance the core offers to the tooth when it is ready. Pasta has a little white dot at the center when it's perfectly cooked; the core loses any residual resistance seconds later, so drain the pasta a few seconds earlier rather than risk overcooking it. And remember: when pasta is al dente, it is more digestible than when it is overcooked, thanks to the carbohydrate bonds which have not yet been broken.

When draining pasta, reserve 1 cup of the cooking water, which can be used to dilute the sauce if needed. Some of the recipes in this book specifically ask that you reserve some of the cooking water; they are those for which the sauce likely requires a bit of cooking water for fluidity.

Never rinse pasta once you have drained it, not even if you want to serve it cold, because the starch that clings to pasta helps the sauce adhere to the pasta and lends flavor. Let the pasta cool, if needed, by spreading it out on a baking sheet.

To combine the pasta and sauce, you can toss the pasta with the sauce in the pan or skillet the sauce is in, return the pasta to the pot from which it was drained and fold in the sauce, or stir the two together in a serving bowl.

Finally, a word about serving your perfectly cooked pasta: a heated bowl is a nice touch, especially if you are serving hot pasta in a cold sauce. To heat a serving bowl, pour a few cups of the pasta cooking water into the bowl, let sit for 30 seconds, then drain before spooning in the pasta. Alternately, preheat the oven to 225° and heat the bowl or platter for 5 minutes.

Giuseppe Ferrara's spicy seafood linguine al cartoccio (recipe on page 108), an unusually sumptuous presentation for pasta.

fabrizio aielli

black farfalle with smoked salmon
and peas • sedanini with rabbit, arugula,
and tomato • capellini with beets, pear,
and lobster • rigatoni with venison
and quince • truffled ditalini

Hailed as a culinary triumph by the Washington, D.C. press and national newspapers, Fabrizio Aielli became enamored with cooking by watching his mother in his family's home kitchen off the coast of Venice. "Everything I cook is an invention of my heart," says Aielli, who owns Goldoni and Teatro Goldoni in Washington, D.C. While at Goldoni he offers his own blend of traditional and contemporary Venetian cuisine, it is at Teatro Goldoni that Fabrizio expresses the full range of his creativity: "I use traditional Italian ingredients, but in new ways. I add spices and herbs that most people don't realize are part of the Italian kitchen, like curry, ginger, and cinnamon, but I do it while respecting the flavors of Italian food." Aielli uses butter and cream sparingly at his restaurants, preferring extra-virgin olive oil for its fruity flavor and many health benefits. When he's not jetting off to Italy for a weekend of culinary inspiration or working on his menus and award-winning wine lists, Aielli likes to spend time with his wife Ingrid, who runs the dining rooms of his restaurants, and play with his two dogs: Sansone, a 185-pound Great Dane, and Dandy, a 4½-pound Yorkie.

black **farfalle** with smoked salmon and peas

As striking visually as it is pleasing to the palate, this extravagant pasta is especially lovely when made with just-picked sweet spring peas. To ensure the smoked salmon tastes fresh and vibrant, stir it in at the very last moment, away from the heat.

serves 4

$2^{1}/_{2}$ cups vegetable broth (see page 184)
$^{1}/_{2}$ Vidalia onion, chopped
4 shallots, chopped
2 cups frozen or shelled fresh peas
$^{1}/_{2}$ cup extra-virgin olive oil
salt and freshly ground black pepper
10 ounces squid ink farfalle
1 tablespoon unsalted butter
7 ounces smoked salmon, julienned

In a saucepan, place the broth, onion, and shallots; cook over high heat until the onion and shallots become tender, about 10 minutes after the broth comes to a boil. Drop in the peas and cook for 2 minutes. Pour the mixture into a blender, and process until it begins to emulsify. Slowly add all but 1 tablespoon of the olive oil while the machine is running, but do not let the mixture become creamy; it should remain fairly thick. Season this pea purée with salt and pepper, and set aside until needed.

Bring 4 quarts of water to a boil. Add the farfalle and salt, and cook until al dente; drain and transfer to a bowl. Fold in the butter, the remaining olive oil, and the smoked salmon. Spoon the pea purée on each of 4 plates, top with the farfalle, and serve hot.

sedanini with rabbit, arugula, and tomato This robust dish is given a light, refreshing flavor and vivacious color thanks to a garnish of arugula and cherry tomatoes.

Heat all but 1 tablespoon of the olive oil in a pan. Add the onion, celery, carrot, and rosemary, and cook until the vegetables are golden, about 10 minutes over medium heat. Stir in the sausage, rabbit, bay leaves, and sage leaves, and cook for 15 minutes, stirring often to brown evenly. Fold in the olives, tomato paste, wine, broth, and garlic; season with salt and pepper, and simmer, uncovered, for 2 hours.

Meanwhile, toss the arugula and cherry tomatoes with the remaining olive oil in a medium bowl, and set aside at room temperature until needed.

Bring 5 quarts of water to a boil, and drop in the sedanini and salt. Cook until the sedanini are al dente; drain.

Return the sedanini to the pot, stir in the rabbit sauce, and toss over medium heat for 1 minute. Spoon onto 4 heated plates, and garnish with the marinated arugula and tomato salad. Serve immediately.

serves 4

3 tablespoons extra-virgin olive oil
1 Vidalia onion, chopped
4 celery stalks, chopped
1 carrot, chopped
1 rosemary sprig
2 ounces Italian sausage,
    casings removed and crumbled
12 ounces ground rabbit
4 bay leaves
4 sage leaves
1/4 cup pitted black olives
2 tablespoons tomato paste
1 1/2 cups dry white wine
2 cups vegetable broth (see page 184)
2 garlic cloves, chopped
salt and freshly ground black pepper
2 bunches arugula, washed,
    stems removed, and chopped
8 ounces cherry tomatoes, halved
1 pound sedanini

capellini with beets, pear, and lobster
Fabrizio tosses the pears with grenadine before roasting them, lending them a lovely pinkish hue and sweet-tart flavor.

Make the beet sauce: Place the beets, pear, and honey in a pot and cover with water. Cook over high heat until the beets are tender, remove from the heat, and pour into a blender. Process the mixture, and add the olive oil in a thin, steady stream while the motor is running to achieve a creamy, emulsified consistency. Set aside.

Make the pears: Preheat the oven to 450°. Place all the ingredients in a baking pan and cover with foil. Bake for 20 minutes.

Make the lobster: Heat the olive oil in a sauté pan and add the lobster; cook for 3 minutes over medium-high heat, deglaze with the brandy and wine, and light a match to the pan (keep your hair and clothes away from the flame). When the flame dies down, add the foie gras and salt, and sauté until cooked, about 5 minutes.

Meanwhile, make the pasta: Bring 4 quarts of water to a boil. Add the capellini and salt, and cook until al dente; drain.

Sauté the capellini in the pan with the lobster for 1 minute over medium-high heat to coat it with the sauce. To serve, ladle some of the beet sauce onto each of 4 plates, place some of the capellini on top, and garnish each serving with half a roasted pear. Serve immediately.

serves 4

For the beet sauce:
3 beets, cubed
1 pear, cubed
2 tablespoons honey
$1/2$ cup extra-virgin olive oil
For the pears:
2 pears, peeled, cored, and halved
2 cups dry white wine
4 garlic cloves, peeled
$1/4$ cup grenadine
3 bay leaves
For the lobster:
2 tablespoons extra-virgin olive oil
1 pound lobster meat
$1/4$ cup brandy
$1/4$ cup dry white wine
5 ounces foie gras, cut into 4 pieces
salt
For the pasta:
10 ounces capellini
salt

rigatoni with venison and quince

The marriage of earthy venison ragù and sweet quince is an ideal one: the ingredients play off one another beautifully, contrasting and merging in a true symphony of flavors. Fabrizio's secret is bittersweet chocolate, which he chops and simmers with the venison and quince.

In a large saucepan, sauté the onion, carrot, and celery in the olive oil until golden and aromatic, about 10 minutes over medium heat. Stir in the pork, venison, bay leaves, and juniper berries, and cook the meat for 15 minutes, or until lightly browned all over, stirring often. Deglaze with the gin and wine, and cook for 5 more minutes. Stir in the quince, tomato paste, broth, rosemary, chocolate, salt, and pepper; bring to a gentle boil and simmer for 2 hours, uncovered. Adjust the salt and pepper.

Meanwhile, bring 5 quarts of water to a boil. Add the rigatoni and salt, and cook until al dente; drain. Return to the pot, fold in the ragù, adjust the seasoning if needed, and serve immediately.

serves 6

1 Vidalia onion, chopped
1 carrot, chopped
4 celery stalks, chopped
$1/2$ cup extra-virgin olive oil
4 ounces ground pork
14 ounces ground venison
4 bay leaves
6 juniper berries
$1/4$ cup gin
$1 1/2$ cups dry red wine
2 quince, chopped
2 tablespoons tomato paste
2 cups vegetable broth (see page 184)
1 rosemary sprig
1 teaspoon bittersweet chocolate, chopped
salt and freshly ground black pepper
1 pound rigatoni

truffled **ditalini** Health-conscious Fabrizio uses a subtle potato purée to give the sauce a creamy consistency without adding any cream at all; the result is both sumptuous and light.

Bring 1 quart of water to a boil and drop in the potato; cook until tender when pierced with a knife, about 20 minutes. Drain, peel, and chop.

In a saucepan, combine the shallot, potato, broth, and $1/8$ teaspoon of the saffron; bring to a boil, and cook over medium heat for 15 minutes. Remove from the heat, and pour into a blender; add the remaining saffron. Process the mixture until it begins to emulsify, then add the olive oil in a thin, steady stream while the motor is running; the texture should be creamy.

Meanwhile, bring 5 quarts of water to a boil. Drop in the asparagus and salt; cook 3 minutes, or until crisp-tender; remove to a bowl of cold water with a slotted spoon. Add the ditalini to the boiling water, and cook until al dente; drain.

In a large sauté pan, toss the ditalini with the potato purée, the drained asparagus, and the Mascarpone for 1 minute over medium heat. Spoon the ditalini onto a serving dish, shave the black truffle over them with a truffle slicer, and serve hot, sprinkled with the Parmigiano.

serves 4

1 potato
1 shallot, chopped
2 cups vegetable broth (see page 184)
$1/4$ teaspoon saffron
$2/3$ cup extra-virgin olive oil
16 pencil-thin asparagus spears, trimmed
salt
1 pound ditalini
1 tablespoon Mascarpone
　(preferably imported Italian)
3 ounces black truffle
$1/3$ cup freshly grated Parmigiano
　Reggiano

paolo alavian

black linguine with diced tuna and fresh tarragon • tagliatelle in pheasant ragù • penne ai quattro formaggi • lobster fusilli with pesto • garganelli with squash, mushrooms, and leeks

It's been five short years since Paolo Alavian opened his first restaurant, Savore, in Manhattan's trendy SoHo with his then-journalist wife Antonia. "My goal at Savore was to serve Tuscan country food, the sort of recipes grandmothers used to cook on big old stoves. I wanted to do a lot of game cookery, pheasant, boar, hare, and so on, and recreate the flavors of Tuscany from sixty, one hundred years ago," says Alavian, who accomplished his goal so successfully that he decided to open two more restaurants over the next four years. At Focacceria L'Ulivo, Paolo's expert pizzaiolo turns out crisp, paper-thin pizzas from a massive wood-burning oven and fragrant, oil-glazed focaccias, while at the more recently opened La Griglia (a joint venture with brother Hadi), Tuscan grilled specialties emerge from the kitchen in tantalizing succession. And Paolo, who has been working with food since he was fourteen, is always near the kitchen to guide his staff and share the tricks that make the difference between a good dish and a great one. "If you really love food, if you love teaching people to cook, you'll never get bored in this business. There's always something new just waiting to be discovered... Like the recipes I've been unearthing in old cookbooks for traditional Tuscan pastas, all hand-made, like pici and pappardelle and all sorts of wonderful ravioli and tortelli, and for pasta sauces like the pheasant ragù we make at Savore. Just when you thought you knew the ultimate way to make something, someone comes along and shows you a whole new way... And sometimes, that someone is a ninety-year-old man who remembers the way his grandfather made a specific dish. The wisdom doesn't always come from the chefs, you know," points out Alavian, adding that his greatest teacher has been his desire to learn as much as possible from others.

black **linguine** with diced tuna and fresh tarragon

Paolo sautés the tuna in this savory, tarragon-laced sauce until it is fully cooked, but says it can also be left medium-rare if you prefer a more tender texture and rosy color to your tuna.

serves 4

1 pound squid ink linguine
salt
$1/3$ cup extra-virgin olive oil
1 leek, white part only,
   cut into $1/4$"-wide strips
8 ounces skinless fresh tuna,
   cut into $1/4$" cubes
$1/2$ cup dry white wine
1 tablespoon minced tarragon
freshly ground black pepper
12 cherry tomatoes, halved

Bring 5 quarts of water to a boil. Drop in the linguine and salt, and cook until al dente; drain, reserving $1/2$ cup of the pasta cooking water.

Meanwhile, heat 2 tablespoons of the olive oil in a skillet. Add the leek and cook until it is translucent and soft, about 5 minutes over medium heat, stirring often.

In a skillet large enough to accommodate the linguine later, heat the remaining olive oil. Add the tuna and sauté until nearly cooked, about 2 minutes over medium-high heat. Deglaze with the wine, and bring to a boil; cook until the wine evaporates, about 2 minutes. Fold in the tarragon, pepper, leek, and cherry tomatoes, and cook for 1 more minute. The tomatoes should still hold together; season with salt.

Toss the linguine into the skillet and sauté for 1 minute to distribute the sauce, adding some of the reserved pasta cooking water if needed to dilute the sauce and give the pasta a slippery texture. Adjust the seasoning, and serve hot.

tagliatelle in pheasant ragù

Paolo, who is known for his rustically elegant game cookery, is very proud of this traditional Tuscan dish. He suggests pappardelle as an alternative to the tagliatelle for anyone who enjoys wide noodles.

Preheat the oven to 375°. Rub the pheasant with 1 tablespoon of the olive oil, season it with salt and pepper, and place it in a stove-to-oven roasting pan; roast for 1 hour, or until the meat comes easily off the bone, basting every 10 minutes with 1 tablespoon of the wine. Remove from the oven and, while it is still warm, pick the meat from the bones with your fingers. Slice it roughly with a sharp knife, and set aside; reserve the bones.

Place the roasting pan on the stove, and brown the pheasant bones in the remaining olive oil over medium heat, stirring often, about 5 minutes. Add the onions, carrots, celery, and garlic, and cook 5 more minutes. Stir in the peppercorns, bay leaf, thyme, parsley, tomato paste, tomatoes, broth, and the remaining wine. Return the roasting pan to the oven and roast until the liquid in the pan has reduced by half, about 25 minutes in all.

Remove the roasting pan from the oven. Strain the liquid in the roasting pan into a saucepan, and reduce it by one-third over medium-high heat. Fold in the sliced pheasant, and cook for 10 minutes.

Meanwhile, bring 5 quarts of water to a boil. Add the tagliatelle and salt, and cook until al dente. Drain. Toss the tagliatelle with the pheasant sauce, adjust the salt if needed, and serve hot.

serves 4

1 pheasant, cleaned and ready to cook
1/4 cup extra-virgin olive oil
salt and freshly ground black pepper
2 cups dry red wine
2 onions, chopped
2 carrots, chopped
2 celery stalks, chopped
1 garlic clove, peeled
1 tablespoon black peppercorns
1 bay leaf
1 thyme sprig
2 Italian parsley sprigs
2 tablespoons tomato paste
1 cup canned strained plum tomatoes
2 cups vegetable broth (see page 184)
1 pound tagliatelle

penne ai quattro formaggi

Literally translated, the name of this dish is penne with four cheeses. But the choice of cheeses is up to you. Paolo likes fresh, creamy goat cheese, luxurious Mascarpone, sharp Tuscan Pecorino, and a touch of blue-veined Gorgonzola—all, of course, topped with freshly grated Parmigiano. So what if it's really five cheeses?

Preheat the oven to 400°. Place the goat cheese, Mascarpone, Pecorino, and Gorgonzola in a bowl set over a pot of gently boiling water, and heat until melted and smooth, about 10 minutes. You should stir the mixture often to prevent if from sticking to the sides of the bowl, and to encourage the four cheeses to melt evenly.

Meanwhile, bring 5 quarts of water to a boil, and add the penne and salt. Halfway into the suggested cooking time, drain the penne and spread them out with a spoon in a buttered roasting pan.

Stir in the melted cheese mixture, fold in the chives, and sprinkle with the Parmigiano. Bake for 30 minutes, or until the penne are golden-brown on the tips and the cheese is bubbling. Serve hot, sprinkled with the pepper if you like.

serves 4

2 ounces fresh goat cheese, cubed
2 ounces Mascarpone
    (preferably imported Italian)
2 ounces freshly grated Tuscan Pecorino
2 ounces Gorgonzola Dolce, cubed
1 pound penne
salt
1 tablespoon unsalted butter
    for greasing the pan
1 bunch chives, snipped
1 cup freshly grated Parmigiano Reggiano
freshly ground black pepper (optional)

lobster **fusilli** with pesto

Maine lobsters have a particularly sweet flavor that Paolo prefers for this succulent pasta. If you are cooking the lobsters rather than buying them already cooked, make a flavorful broth for poaching them: bring 12 quarts of water to a boil with 1 cup of dry white wine, 1 bay leaf, 2 thyme sprigs, 1 onion, 1 garlic clove, and 1 teaspoon of black peppercorns, and cook for 20 minutes before dropping in the lobsters.

serves 4

1 tablespoon pine nuts
2 garlic cloves, 1 peeled and 1 crushed
4 bunches basil, leaves only
$1/4$ cup freshly grated Pecorino Romano
$1/4$ cup freshly grated Parmigiano
  Reggiano
1 cup plus 2 tablespoons extra-virgin
  olive oil
1 pound fusilli
salt
$2^1/2$ pounds lobster meat, cooked and
  cleaned, cut into $1/8$"-thick medallions

Heat a small skillet over medium heat. Add the pine nuts and cook, stirring constantly, until toasted all over, about 3 minutes. Place the pine nuts in a mortar, and add the peeled garlic clove; crush with a pestle until a paste forms. Remove and set aside; place the basil in the mortar, and crush until a paste also forms. Combine the pine nut mixture, basil, Pecorino, and Parmigiano in a bowl, and slowly add 1 cup of the olive oil, whisking. The pesto should be nearly smooth. (The pesto can be made 24 hours ahead and refrigerated, covered with olive oil to prevent it from blackening.)

Bring 5 quarts of water to a boil. Add the fusilli and salt, and cook until al dente. Drain, reserving $1/2$ cup of the pasta cooking water.

Meanwhile, in a sauté pan large enough to hold the fusilli later, heat the remaining olive oil. Add the crushed garlic clove, and cook over medium heat for 30 seconds, or until golden; discard the garlic. Add the lobster medallions to the pan, and cook 30 seconds to infuse the lobster with the garlic-scented olive oil. Fold in the fusilli. Remove from the heat, and turn out into a bowl; stir in the pesto, adjust the salt, dilute with some of the reserved pasta cooking water if necessary, and serve hot.

garganelli with squash, mushrooms, and leeks

A favorite at Paolo's La Griglia. This pasta should be savored by a fireplace on snug autumn evenings. Paolo uses a combination of porcini, chanterelle, and lobster mushrooms, but suggests that you use whatever is freshest and most fragrant at your market and says that a few dried porcini can also be incorporated into the sauce.

In a sauté pan large enough to hold the garganelli later, cook the leeks in 2 tablespoons of the olive oil until they become translucent, about 5 minutes over medium heat. Fold in the cubed squash, and cook until it becomes tender, about 10 minutes, stirring often to cook evenly.

In another pan, brown the garlic cloves in the remaining olive oil; discard the garlic, and add the porcini, chanterelle, and lobster mushrooms. Cook for 3 minutes without stirring over medium-high heat; the mushrooms should be cooked quickly, over intense heat, so they do not release water. Season with salt and pepper, and fold into the leek and squash in the first pan.

Meanwhile, bring 5 quarts of water to a boil. Add the garganelli and salt, and cook until the garganelli are al dente; drain. Fold the garganelli into the sauce in the pan, and toss over medium heat for 1 minute to mingle the flavors. Adjust the seasoning if needed, and serve the garganelli immediately.

serves 4

2 leeks, white part only,
  cut into $1/4$"-wide strips
$1/4$ cup extra-virgin olive oil
$1/2$ butternut squash, cut into $1/2$" cubes
2 garlic cloves, crushed
4 ounces porcini mushrooms,
  scrubbed and diced
4 ounces chanterelle mushrooms,
  scrubbed and diced
4 ounces lobster mushrooms,
  scrubbed and diced
salt and freshly ground black pepper
1 pound garganelli

franco
barone

fusilli with tomato filets • sicilian timballo • orecchiette and broccoli raab • tagliatelle and vegetable medley • spaghettini with mussels and clams

Born in Sicily and raised in Milan, Franco Barone didn't need to attend culinary school: he developed his sense of taste and his chef's touch under the tutelage of his uncle, who owned a restaurant in Milan. "My uncle taught me everything I needed to get started: he taught me how to select ingredients, how to respect them, how to draw the most flavor from them, without masking their essential flavors." Today, as Executive Chef at Antonello's in Santa Ana, California, Franco draws on this love for primary ingredients to create a cuisine that is a skillful blend of the regional and the innovative. "Every region of Italy offers distinct flavors, and the same dish can be made dozens of different ways across Italy. And even though at Antonello's I do more Piedmontese cuisine, I like to put specials from other regions on the menu." Using seasonal foods as his guide and his muse, Franco recreates regional Italian recipes for his clientele; one of his favorites is orecchiette tossed with garlicky rapini, an Apulian dish that he calls "comfort food at its best." Another is a classic timballo stuffed with penne, hard-boiled eggs, meatballs, and mozzarella, which he cooks to celebrate his Sicilian roots. But Franco also goes beyond the tenets of regional Italian cooking, and creates vibrant dishes like ravioli stuffed with porcini or tagliatelle tossed with ribbons of fresh vegetables.

fusilli with tomato filets This dish

embodies the Italian spirit of simplicity: only ripe tomatoes, fruity olive oil, a hint of garlic, and fragrant basil marry to create a flavorful, summery sauce for fusilli. Use penne rigate or capellini instead of fusilli if you prefer, and pass some freshly grated Pecorino at the table for those who want it.

Bring 5 quarts of water to a boil. Make a cross on the bottom of each tomato and drop into the water; cook 1 minute. Remove with a slotted spoon to a bowl filled with cold water and reserve the boiling water in the pot to cook the pasta later. Slip the peels off the tomatoes, cut off the stem end, and cut in half. Scoop out the seeds and cut the tomatoes into a julienne with a sharp knife.

Heat a medium sauté pan and add the olive oil and garlic; cook until the garlic is aromatic, about 30 seconds, then stir in the basil and tomatoes. Cook 5 minutes over medium heat.

Meanwhile, cook the fusilli with salt in the reserved boiling water until al dente. Drain; toss the fusilli with the sauce, and serve hot.

serves 6

6 ripe plum tomatoes
2 tablespoons extra-virgin olive oil
4 garlic cloves, chopped
12 basil leaves, torn
1 pound fusilli
salt

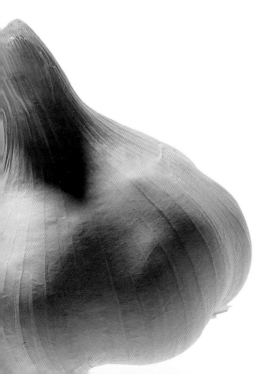

sicilian **timballo** This elegant first course encloses
homemade meatballs, hard-boiled eggs, mozzarella, sausage, and penne in a delicate
pasta casing. The timballo can be prepared (but not baked) up to 24 hours ahead;
bake it just before serving, and allow it to rest for 5 minutes before unmolding.

serves 12

For the sauce:
$^1/_2$ cup extra-virgin olive oil
2 onions, chopped
1 pound Italian sausage, crumbled
1 cup dry red wine
1 cup tomato paste
10 cups canned strained plum tomatoes
$^1/_2$ cup basil leaves
1 tablespoon salt
1 tablespoon sugar
1 teaspoon freshly ground black pepper

For the meatballs:
1 pound ground veal
$^1/_4$ cup freshly grated Parmigiano Reggiano
3 garlic cloves, minced
1 tablespoon chopped Italian parsley
$^1/_2$ teaspoon salt
$^1/_2$ teaspoon freshly ground black pepper
3 eggs

For the timballo:
6 lasagna sheets
salt
24 ounces penne
1 tablespoon olive oil for greasing
1 cup freshly grated Parmigiano Reggiano
1 cup grated mozzarella
8 hard-boiled eggs, quartered
4 basil sprigs

Make the sauce: In a large pot, heat the olive oil. Add the onions and sauté for 10 minutes over medium-high heat. Stir in the sausage and cook for 3 minutes, stirring. Deglaze with the wine; cook for 2 minutes. Add the tomato paste, tomatoes, basil, salt, sugar, and pepper; bring to a boil, then simmer, covered, for 20 minutes.

Meanwhile, make the meatballs: Place the ground veal in a medium bowl; add all the remaining ingredients and mix well. Shape into small balls; drop into the sauce. Cook for 10 to 15 minutes longer; remove from the heat and cool.

Assemble the timballo: Preheat the oven to 425°. Bring 7 quarts of water to a boil. Add the lasagna and salt, and cook until al dente; remove with a slotted spoon to a bowl of cold water. Add the penne to the boiling water; cook until al dente, drain, and place in a bowl. Line an oiled ovenproof 9" oval mold with the lasagna sheets, draining them and blotting them dry first. Add the Parmigiano, mozzarella, eggs, and sauce to the penne in the bowl. Spoon the penne mixture inside the lasagna-lined mold and cover with the overhanging lasagna sheets. Place the mold in a large roasting pan filled halfway with water. Bake for 35 minutes. Cool for 5 minutes. Flip the mold over onto a platter, unmold the timballo, and serve, garnished with the basil.

orecchiette and broccoli raab

Sicilian-born Franco Barone loves this classic Apulian dish "because the flavors are so sunny, so direct, so Mediterranean." He suggests adding 2 salted anchovies (gutted and rinsed) to the garlic in the olive oil for extra flavor.

Trim the broccoli raab, removing any yellow leaves and snipping off the tough lower stems. Wash in cool water. Bring 5 quarts of water to a boil. Add the broccoli raab and cook for 5 minutes, or until crisp-tender. Remove the broccoli raab with a slotted spoon to a bowl of cold water; return the water to a boil.

Add the orecchiette and salt to the boiling water, and cook until al dente; drain. (Check the package for cooking time: orecchiette usually take 15 to 20 minutes.)

Meanwhile, heat 2 tablespoons of the olive oil in a large sauté pan. Add the garlic and chili, and cook until the garlic is golden. Add the broccoli raab, draining it well first and squeezing out some of the excess water; sauté for 3 minutes.

Toss the orecchiette with the broccoli raab in the pan. Season with salt, drizzle with the remaining olive oil, and serve immediately.

serves 6

1 bunch broccoli raab
1 pound orecchiette
salt
½ cup extra-virgin olive oil
2 garlic cloves, sliced
1 dried chili pepper, crumbled

tagliatelle and vegetable medley

The ultimate vegetarian recipe for spring, when sweet peas are in season and light, vibrant flavors refresh the spirit and soothe the mind. Franco suggests using flat-leaf spinach rather than curly for the sauce, since its texture is a little more delicate.

Bring 5 quarts of water to a boil. Add the tagliatelle and salt, and cook until the tagliatelle are al dente. Drain, reserving 1 cup of the pasta cooking water.

Meanwhile, heat the olive oil in a pan that will accommodate the tagliatelle later. Cook the shallots until they are golden brown around the edges, about 3 minutes over medium heat. Fold in the zucchini, yellow squash, carrots, peas, and spinach, and sauté for 3 more minutes; the vegetables should be wilted but not soft.

Toss the tagliatelle with the vegetables in the pan, and cook for 1 minute to mingle the flavors. Add a little of the reserved pasta cooking water to dilute the sauce if necessary, and adjust the salt before transferring to a heated platter. Serve hot.

serves 6

1 pound tagliatelle
salt
3 tablespoons extra-virgin olive oil
2 shallots, chopped
1/2 cup julienned zucchini
1/2 cup julienned yellow squash
1/2 cup julienned carrots
1/2 cup frozen or shelled fresh peas
1/2 cup julienned fresh spinach

spaghettini with mussels and clams

Franco sometimes uses fresh plum tomatoes to make this zesty seafood sauce; you can use canned tomatoes for ease if you prefer.

Scrub the mussels and remove the beards with a paring knife. Place in a bowl; add cold water to cover and 1 tablespoon of salt, and soak for 30 minutes; drain and rinse. In another bowl, soak the clams with 1 tablespoon of salt and cold water to cover for 30 minutes; drain and rinse.

Bring 5 quarts of water to a boil. Add the spaghettini and salt, and cook until the spaghettini are al dente; drain.

Meanwhile, heat the olive oil in a medium pan. Cook the garlic until it becomes golden, about 30 seconds; add the mussels, clams, basil, parsley, and wine. Cook for 5 minutes, or until the wine has nearly evaporated, then add the clam juice or fish broth and tomatoes, and simmer for 5 minutes.

Toss the spaghettini with the mussel and clam sauce. Season with salt and pepper (remember that the mussels and clams are quite salty, so be sparing), and serve hot.

serves 6

20 black mussels
salt
20 Manila clams
1 pound spaghettini
$^{1}/_{2}$ cup extra-virgin olive oil
4 garlic cloves, sliced
12 basil leaves, torn
2 tablespoons chopped Italian parsley
1 cup dry white wine
1 cup clam juice or fish broth
  (see page 184)
3 cups canned strained plum tomatoes
freshly ground black pepper

Roberto Zeballos-Peralda

gorgonzola and porcini fusilli • bucatini in rich tomato-pancetta sauce • pennette portofino • rigatoni in duck sauce • mezze penne alla checca

roberto **bernardoni**

Ask Roberto to describe himself, and the first word out of his mouth will be "Florentine". The second will surely be "Chef". Roberto Bernardoni, Florentine chef and food enthusiast, came to the world of cooking late: he was thirty-one when he decided to leave his civil service job in Florence and open his first restaurant, Ganino, with his family. Soon after Roberto experienced success with Ganino, he opened L'Osteria delle Tre Panche with his current wife Patrizia. In 1991, Roberto moved to California, where he fulfilled a lifelong dream of running a restaurant in America. At La Strada, which is located in the historic Gaslamp Quarter of San Diego, Roberto continues to offer his public the same traditional Tuscan dishes that won him a loyal following in Florence: summer brings spaghetti with saffron, cream, and zucchini blossoms, winter brings rigatoni in a hearty duck sauce. Roberto soon opened La Strada Bonita, and sold his restaurants in Florence to focus entirely on California. "Once a Florentine, always a Florentine. I may live in California now, but it's what I learned to eat and to cook with my grandmother Alba that defines who I am. I go back to Florence every six months at the most, and I fill my nose and mouth with the scents and flavors of home." Roberto credits his grandmother with teaching him to cook, and says it is through watching her that he learned the secret to great food: "It's all about simplicity. Food can become very complicated if you let it. But keeping it simple—keeping it genuine—takes real expertise."

gorgonzola and porcini
fusilli
Being a native Tuscan, Roberto loves porcini mushrooms, and he uses them in a number of his favorite pastas. This dish mingles the pungent yet creamy flavor of Gorgonzola with the earthy aroma of porcini, resulting in a memorable first course.

Melt the butter in a large skillet over medium heat and add the shallot. Cook for 2 minutes, then add the porcini. Season with salt and pepper, and cook for 3 more minutes. Pour in the cream and stir in the Gorgonzola, and cook until the Gorgonzola has melted into the sauce, about 2 minutes.

Meanwhile, bring 5 quarts of water to a boil, and cook the fusilli with salt until al dente. Drain, reserving 1/3 cup of the pasta cooking water, and pour the fusilli into the skillet with the sauce, stirring well.

Fold in the parsley and the Parmigiano. If the sauce seems a bit too dry, stir in a bit of the reserved pasta cooking water. Adjust the seasoning if needed, and serve hot.

serves 4

4 tablespoons unsalted butter
1 shallot, minced
5 ounces porcini, scrubbed and julienned
salt and freshly ground black pepper
1 cup heavy cream
4 ounces Gorgonzola Dolce, cubed
1 pound fusilli
1 teaspoon minced Italian parsley
1/2 cup freshly grated Parmigiano Reggiano

bucatini in rich tomato-pancetta sauce

Called bucatini all'amatriciana, this pasta is a staple in Roman trattorias. In Italy, guanciale, the cured meat from the cheek of a pig, is used rather than the more ordinary pancetta. Avoid bacon, however, since it is smoked and gives the dish a completely different flavor.

Heat the olive oil in a heavy saucepan and add the pancetta. Cook over medium-low heat until the pancetta takes on a little color without burning, about 10 minutes. Stir in the onion and cook just until it is wilted and golden, then add the tomatoes, salt, and chili pepper or freshly ground black pepper, and cook over moderately high heat until the sauce reduces, about 20 minutes.

Meanwhile, bring 5 quarts of water to a boil. Add the bucatini and salt and cook until al dente; drain. Toss with the amatriciana sauce, transfer to a heated serving dish, and sprinkle with the Pecorino. Serve hot, passing additional Pecorino at the table.

serves 4

$1/4$ cup extra-virgin olive oil
4 ounces pancetta, cubed
$1/2$ onion, minced
3 cups canned chopped plum tomatoes
salt
1 dried chili pepper, crumbled (optional),
　or freshly ground black pepper
1 pound bucatini
$1/2$ cup freshly grated Pecorino Romano,
　plus extra

pennette portofino Named after the

splendid Ligurian town of Portofino, where the rich and famous dock their yachts and holiday, this sultry shrimp pasta is laced with vodka and crushed red pepper.

serves 4

$^1/_2$ cup extra-virgin olive oil
10 jumbo shrimp, shelled and deveined
3 garlic cloves, minced
2 tablespoons chopped Italian parsley
salt and freshly ground black pepper
$^1/_8$ teaspoon crushed red pepper
$^1/_3$ cup vodka
2 cups tomato sauce (see page 185)
$^1/_4$ cup heavy cream
1 pound pennette rigate

In a sauté pan large enough to accommodate the pennette later, heat the olive oil and sauté the shrimp until they just turn pink, about 2 minutes over medium-high heat. Reduce the heat to medium, add the garlic, parsley, salt, pepper, and crushed red pepper, and cook for 1 minute. Pour in the vodka and light a match to the pan, keeping your hair and clothes away from the flame. As soon as the flame dies down, add the tomato sauce, and cook for 3 more minutes. Stir in the cream, bring to a gentle boil, and cook 2 more minutes.

Meanwhile, bring 5 quarts of water to a boil. Add the pennette and salt, and cook until they are al dente; drain and sauté with the sauce for 1 minute, adjusting the salt if needed. Serve the pennette immediately.

rigatoni in duck sauce Roberto's
variation on Tuscany's famed pappardelle in duck sauce, and just as delicious. Look for duck at specialty shops and butchers with a selection of exotic meats.

Heat the olive oil in a deep saucepan and add the carrot, onion, celery, and bay leaves; cook over medium heat for 5 minutes, or until the vegetables start to soften and become aromatic. While the vegetables cook down, cut the duck into 8 pieces.

Add the duck to the vegetables in the pot. Raise the heat to medium-high, and cook until the duck browns on both sides, turning once; it will take about 7 minutes. Pour in the wine and allow it to evaporate. Lower the heat to medium, and cook the sauce for another 20 to 25 minutes, stirring once in a while; the duck should not be tender yet. Turn off the heat under the pot.

Remove the duck pieces from the pot, cool until the pieces can be touched without burning the fingers, and bone them; chop the meat into 1/4" pieces. Return the diced duck to the pot, add the tomatoes and 1 cup of water, and cook over medium-low heat for 1 more hour. Season with salt.

While the sauce finishes cooking, bring 5 quarts of water to a boil. Add the rigatoni and salt, and cook until al dente; drain. Return the rigatoni to the pot, fold in the duck sauce, and heat for 2 minutes. Serve hot.

serves 4

1/2 cup extra-virgin olive oil
1 carrot, chopped
1 onion, chopped
1 celery stalk, chopped
2 bay leaves
one 5-pound duck, skinned,
    extra fat removed
1 cup dry red wine
1 cup canned chopped plum tomatoes
salt
1 pound rigatoni

mezze penne alla checca

This refreshing Tuscan dish uses green tomatoes to advantage; their pronounced acidity is balanced by Tuscany's fruity extra-virgin olive oil.

In a large pan, heat the olive oil and add the garlic. When the garlic begins to take on a faint golden color, immediately turn off the flame and add the cubed red and green tomatoes, the basil, and salt and pepper to the garlic-infused olive oil. The sauce should be slightly tart from the green tomatoes.

Meanwhile, bring 5 quarts of water to a boil and drop in the mezze penne and salt; cook until al dente, and drain. Stir the mezze penne into the sauce, adjust the seasoning if necessary, and serve hot, topped with the shaved Parmigiano.

serves 4

$1/2$ cup extra-virgin olive oil
3 garlic cloves, halved
8 ounces red Roma tomatoes, cubed
8 ounces green Roma tomatoes, cubed
12 basil leaves, torn
salt and freshly ground black pepper
1 pound mezze penne
$1/4$ cup shaved Parmigiano Reggiano

giuseppe
casadio

garganelli with pancetta, peas, and cream • trofie with pesto, potatoes, and beans • spaghetti alla puttanesca • tagliatelle alla carbonara • linguine with mussels

Perhaps it's because of the climate that Ligurian-born Giuseppe Casadio finally settled in Florida after years of working the world's top cruise lines. That, and his desire to make his mark on the local food scene. "When I arrived in Florida back in the late seventies, the Italian restaurants had a long way to go. I saw that there was a lot of potential, and so I got down to business," he explains. Giuseppe opened his first restaurant, Ristorante Casadio, in 1980. Four years later, he launched Osteria Italian Restaurant and Piccirilli Italian Restaurant. A gourmet store followed, as did a fourth restaurant called Cuoco Matto (The Crazy Cook) and a fifth called Coco Bello. Today, Casadio focuses his energy on Cuoco Matto and Osteria, both in Sarasota. Despite his restaurant's name, there is nothing crazy about the way Giuseppe cooks: "What I learned on the cruise lines and in my early days cooking on the Italian Riviera is discipline, presentation, and the importance of consistency. If you come into my restaurant and enjoy the trofie al pesto one day—one of my favorite dishes, since I'm from Liguria, the birthplace of trofie and pesto—then you can be sure you'll enjoy it the next time. I'd rather not even put pesto on my menu if the basil isn't fragrant. Then I really would be crazy," he adds with a laugh.

garganelli with pancetta, peas, and cream This dish is also

wonderful with penne if garganelli are hard to find in your area. Giuseppe sometimes substitutes Prosciutto for the pancetta for a slightly different flavor.

In a pan large enough to accommodate the garganelli later, heat the butter and olive oil. Add the onion, and cook until it begins to wilt, about 5 minutes over medium heat. Fold in the peas. Cook over medium-low heat for 10 minutes, and stir in the pancetta. Cook for 2 minutes, or until the pancetta starts to render its fat. Pour in the cream, and bring to a boil, then simmer for 3 more minutes; the sauce should be rather thick in consistency at this point.

Meanwhile, bring 4 quarts of water to a boil. Add the garganelli and salt, and cook until al dente. Drain, and toss with the sauce in the pan; stir in the Parmigiano, adjust the salt if necessary, and serve.

serves 4

2 tablespoons unsalted butter
2 tablespoons extra-virgin olive oil
1 onion, thinly sliced
1 cup frozen or shelled fresh peas
2 ounces pancetta, diced
$^1/_2$ cup heavy cream
12 ounces garganelli
salt
1 cup freshly grated Parmigiano Reggiano

trofie with pesto, potatoes, and beans

Famous in the town of Recco, near Giuseppe's birthplace in Liguria, this pasta is a taste of summer on a plate.

serves 6

2 tablespoons pine nuts
1 bunch tender basil, leaves only
1 garlic clove, peeled
$1/2$ teaspoon sea salt, plus extra
$1/2$ cup extra-virgin olive oil
2 tablespoons freshly grated Parmigiano Reggiano
2 tablespoons freshly grated Pecorino Romano
2 potatoes, cut into $1/4$" cubes
8 ounces baby string beans, tipped
1 pound trofie

Toast the pine nuts to release their flavor by placing them on a baking sheet and baking them for 5 to 10 minutes in a preheated 375° oven. Make the pesto: Place the basil, garlic, toasted pine nuts, and sea salt in a food processor. Pulse to blend. Slowly add the olive oil in a thin, steady stream while the processor is running; process until nearly smooth, then transfer to a bowl. Fold in the Parmigiano and Pecorino with a fork; this helps preserve some texture.

Meanwhile, bring 6 quarts of water to a boil. Add the potatoes, string beans, trofie, and salt, and cook until the trofie are al dente; the potatoes and string beans should be tender. Drain, reserving 1 cup of the pasta cooking water. Return the trofie to the pot, and fold in the pesto; add as much of the reserved pasta cooking water as needed to dilute the pesto to a coating consistency, adjust the salt, and serve immediately.

spaghetti alla puttanesca

The name of this favorite pasta dish is derived from puttana, a colloquial term for "ladies of the night". It's speculated that the sauce earned its name because of its spicy flavor. Another theory holds that the name has to do with how quickly the sauce can be put together, the reasoning being that since it cooks so quickly, even women with a very busy work schedule (!) have the time to prepare it.

Heat the olive oil in a saucepan. Add the garlic and mash it with a fork to release its aroma. After 1 minute, add the chili and cook until aromatic, about 30 seconds. Stir in the anchovies and mash them with a fork to break them up into the oil; cook for 1 minute. Stir in the tomatoes, olives, capers, and tomato paste; cook over high heat, uncovered, until slightly reduced, about 10 minutes. You don't need to add salt to the sauce since the capers, olives, and anchovies are quite salty.

 Meanwhile, bring 5 quarts of water to a boil. Add the spaghetti and salt, and cook until al dente; drain. Toss the spaghetti with the sauce in a serving bowl, and serve hot.

serves 4

5 tablespoons extra-virgin olive oil
1 garlic clove, crushed
1 dried chili pepper, crumbled
6 salted anchovies, rinsed and deboned
3 cups canned chopped plum tomatoes
1 cup pitted black olives
$1/4$ cup salted capers, rinsed
2 teaspoons tomato paste
1 pound spaghetti
salt

tagliatelle alla carbonara

A specialty from Rome. The garlic in the dish is optional, says Giuseppe; it adds an aromatic note, but can be omitted if you prefer. Be sure to buy organic eggs for the carbonara sauce, since they will barely be cooked.

serves 4

2 tablespoons unsalted butter
4 ounces pancetta, diced
1 garlic clove, peeled
2 eggs
1 pound tagliatelle
salt
$1/2$ cup freshly grated Pecorino Romano
$1/2$ cup freshly grated Parmigiano Reggiano
1 teaspoon cracked black pepper

In a large saucepan, heat the butter until it melts over medium heat. Add the pancetta and garlic, and cook until the pancetta is golden; discard the garlic, and set the pan aside. In a small bowl, whisk the eggs until they are completely creamy.

Meanwhile, bring 5 quarts of water to a boil. Add the tagliatelle and salt, and cook until al dente. Drain.

Toss the tagliatelle with the butter and pancetta in the pan. Remove from the heat and pour in the beaten eggs, stirring constantly to avoid curdling and to coat the pasta well. Add $1/4$ cup of the Pecorino, $1/4$ cup of the Parmigiano, and the cracked black pepper, and stir to coat thoroughly. Stir in the remaining Pecorino and Parmigiano, transfer to a serving platter, and serve hot.

linguine with mussels
Simplicity itself, this seafood pasta reminds Giuseppe of his childhood near Genoa. Giuseppe suggests adding a splash of dry white wine to the mussels as they cook if you like.

Clean the mussels by brushing them under cool running water. Pull off any beards, and place in a bowl; cover with cold water, add 1 tablespoon of salt, and soak for 30 minutes, then drain.

Heat the olive oil in a sauté pan large enough to hold the linguine later, and add the garlic; cook until golden and aromatic, about 45 seconds over medium heat. Add the mussels and cook for 5 minutes, or until they all open; as they open, remove each one from the pan, and delicately extract each mussel from within its shell; discard the shells. Strain the mussel cooking juices through a filter-lined sieve, and return to the pan along with the mussels.

Meanwhile, bring 4 quarts of water to a boil. Add the linguine and salt, and cook until al dente. Drain, and toss into the pan with the mussels. Carefully, with 2 forks, lift and immerse the linguine in the sauce to mingle the flavors. Season with salt and pepper, and sprinkle with the parsley. Transfer the pasta to a serving dish, and serve hot.

serves 4

2 pounds mussels
salt
1 cup extra-virgin olive oil
2 garlic cloves, minced
12 ounces linguine
freshly ground black pepper
1 tablespoon minced Italian parsley

Joe Greene

ralph
conte

bucatini with roasted peppers and olives
• ditalini with escarole, beans, and
sausage • capellini and lobster fradiavolo
• black tagliatelle in squid sauce •
linguine in clam sauce

Generous portions, progressive regional cuisine, and dramatic presentation are what Ralph Conte, Executive Chef and owner of Providence, Rhode Island's Raphael Bar Risto and Tunnel Bar Raphael, delivers to fans who come from near and far for a taste of his creations. Born and raised in Cranston, Conte knew he wanted to make food his career by his late teens. He trained in Italy, and returned to America at twenty-three, where he worked his way up from cooking pasta in a neighborhood café to overseeing the sprawling waterfront restaurant that bears his name. Ralph and his wife and partner Elisa attribute their success to Ralph's bold approach to Italian cuisine. Ralph was among the first chefs to make wood-fire cooking his trademark, and offered dessert pizzas when few people had heard of them. "I'm not afraid of taking risks, trying new things. I'd rather put on a show than bore my clients with the same stuff they can find everywhere else. So my signature dishes are big-ticket items like capellini with lobster fradiavolo, gnocchi with flaming shrimp in vodka sauce. Why just cook a lobster and drape it over pasta when you can make the dish sing?"

bucatini with roasted peppers and olives

Bold, vivacious, and sunny, this dish evokes the feeling of summer by the sea in Italy. Ralph sometimes combines roasted red, orange, and yellow peppers for extra color.

Preheat the broiler. Line a baking sheet with aluminum foil and place the pepper on it; broil until blistered on all sides and blackened all over, turning 3 times, for about 20 minutes. Remove from the oven, wrap in the aluminum foil, and cool to room temperature. Unwrap, peel, seed, and slice the roasted pepper. Set aside.

Bring 5 quarts of water to a boil, add the bucatini and salt, and cook until the bucatini are al dente; drain.

Meanwhile, in a pan large enough to accommodate the bucatini later, heat the olive oil and add the garlic; cook until light brown, about 30 seconds over medium heat. Stir in the black olives and the Sicilian olives, and cook for 2 minutes; add the roasted pepper, 1 cup of water, and the anchovies, and simmer for 5 more minutes.

Toss the bucatini into the sauce in the pan, cook for 2 minutes, and fold in the capers, bread crumbs, basil, and pepper. Spoon onto 4 heated plates, garnish with the parsley, and serve hot.

serves 4

1 red pepper
1 pound bucatini
salt
$1/4$ cup extra-virgin olive oil
6 garlic cloves, sliced
12 dry-cured black olives, pitted
12 Sicilian green olives, pitted
6 anchovy filets
2 tablespoons capers
$3/4$ cup fresh bread crumbs
$1/4$ cup basil leaves, torn
freshly ground black pepper
4 Italian parsley sprigs

ditalini with escarole, beans, and sausage

Nutritious and energizing, this robust pasta is as comforting as a bowl of soup on a drizzly autumn night. Ralph plays with a traditional Italian trio—beans, escarole, and sausage—and livens it up by adding a pinch of ground red pepper, a generous dose of freshly ground black pepper, and some fruity extra-virgin olive oil.

In a large pot, heat 2 tablespoons of the olive oil and add the sliced garlic and onion; cook until translucent, about 5 minutes over medium heat. Fold in the escarole and sausage, and sauté until the escarole begins to wilt, about 5 minutes. Pour in the broth, and simmer for 30 minutes, stirring every 5 minutes or so to prevent sticking.

Add the cannellini beans, crushed red pepper, black pepper, and salt, and simmer 20 more minutes, still stirring every few minutes. Stir the ditalini into the pot, and continue to cook for 10 more minutes. Meanwhile, toast the bread until it is golden brown, and rub it with the remaining garlic clove.

When the dish is done, it should resemble a stew more than a soup. Serve hot, drizzled with the remaining olive oil and accompanied by the garlic-rubbed bread.

serves 4

¼ cup extra-virgin olive oil
7 garlic cloves, 6 sliced and 1 peeled
1 onion, diced
1 head escarole, washed
    and cut into 2"-wide strips
1 pound Italian sausage,
    casings removed and crumbled
2 cups chicken broth (see page 183)
one 16-ounce can cannellini beans,
    drained and rinsed
1 teaspoon crushed red pepper
1 teaspoon freshly ground black pepper
salt
8 ounces ditalini
4 slices country bread

capellini and lobster fradiavolo

This sensational pasta is Ralph's number-one selling dish. Fans come for a taste of it from as far away as Boston and Connecticut.

serves 4

two 1-pound lobsters
$^1/_2$ cup extra-virgin olive oil
1 onion, julienned
1 teaspoon capers
8 Sicilian olives, pitted
4 garlic cloves, minced
2 teaspoons chili flakes
$1^1/_2$ cups dry white wine
6 tomatoes, peeled, seeded, and chopped
2 oregano sprigs, leaves only, minced
salt and freshly ground black pepper
1 pound capellini
1 bunch basil, leaves only, torn

Bring 10 quarts of water to a boil, drop in the lobsters, and cook for 12 minutes. Drain and cool. Remove the meat from the claws and tail, and be sure to reserve the juice and head for the sauce. In a sauté pan, heat the olive oil. Add the onion, capers, olives, and garlic, and cook over high heat until the onion becomes translucent, about 3 minutes. Add the chili flakes and wine, and reduce the heat to a simmer. Fold in the tomatoes and oregano, and simmer for 10 minutes. Stir in the meat from the lobster, as well as the reserved lobster juice and the lobster head, and cook for 2 more minutes. Season with salt and pepper. Remove the head and reserve it for the garnish.

Meanwhile, bring 5 quarts of water to a boil. Add the capellini and salt, and cook until al dente; drain. Toss gently with the sauce, and top with the basil. Serve hot, garnished with the reserved lobster head.

black **tagliatelle** in squid sauce

When buying squid, select smaller specimens: they are softer and less rubbery than large squid. In this dish, they are cooked in tomato sauce with plenty of garlic and chili flakes; the drizzle of squid ink ties the flavors together.

Heat the olive oil in a large pan, and cook the garlic until it is just golden brown around the edges, about 30 seconds over medium heat. Add the chili flakes and cook for 10 more seconds, then fold in the squid and sauté for 1 minute. Deglaze the pan with the wine and cook until the liquid reduces by half, about 1 minute. Stir in the tomatoes and reduce by one-third, then add the squid ink and stir to mix well.

Meanwhile, bring 5 quarts of water to a boil, and add the tagliatelle and salt; cook until al dente. Drain, and toss the tagliatelle into the pan with the squid sauce. Sauté for 1 minute, adjust the seasoning if needed, fold in the basil and parsley, and spoon into 4 heated bowls. Top with the caviar and serve hot.

serves 4

1 tablespoon extra-virgin olive oil
4 garlic cloves, sliced
1/2 teaspoon chili flakes
8 ounces cleaned squid, bodies cut
   into rings and tentacles halved
2 tablespoons dry white wine
1/2 cup canned chopped plum tomatoes
1/4 cup squid ink
1 pound squid ink tagliatelle
salt
1 tablespoon minced basil
1 tablespoon minced Italian parsley
1 ounce Sevruga caviar

linguine in clam sauce
Ralph tosses fresh oregano and an abundant dose of garlic into this classic seafood pasta. If you prefer, you can omit the tomatoes and serve your linguine in bianco instead, adding Italian parsley instead of basil to the sauce.

Place the clams in a bowl, add water to cover, and pour in 1 tablespoon of salt; set aside to soak for 30 minutes. Drain and rinse under running water; this step gets rid of any impurities and sand in the clams.

Heat ⅓ cup of the olive oil in a large sauté pan, and add the garlic and clams; cook over medium heat until the garlic browns, about 1 minute. Stir in the tomatoes, wine, salt, pepper, and oregano, and cover. Simmer for 10 minutes, or until the clams open. Discard any unopened clams.

Meanwhile, bring 5 quarts of water to a boil. Add the linguine and salt, and cook until al dente; drain. Toss the linguine with the clam sauce, adjust the salt if needed, and fold in the basil. Spoon the linguine into 4 heated bowls and serve hot, drizzled with the remaining olive oil.

serves 4

24 littleneck clams
salt
½ cup extra-virgin olive oil
12 garlic cloves, sliced
4 ripe tomatoes, cut into ¼" cubes
1 cup dry white wine
freshly ground black pepper
12 oregano sprigs, leaves only, chopped
1 pound linguine
1 bunch basil, leaves only, julienned

francesco
crescenzo

bucatini with sardines and fennel •
springtime orecchini • pappardelle with
porcini, chicken livers, and tomatoes •
pasta e fagioli alla napoletana • rigatoni
with creamy fontina sauce

Born on the Amalfi Coast, the stretch that has been called the world's most beautiful coastline, Francesco Crescenzo was lucky enough to experience the incredible scope of Italian cuisine first-hand: "When I was young, my family moved to Castelfranco Veneto, near Treviso. I already had a pretty good appreciation for good food, but in the Veneto, I learned about the local cuisine. I grew immensely as a result of my exposure to Northern Italian cuisine." Knowing he wanted to be a chef early on, Francesco attended culinary school in the Veneto, then started cooking in top kitchens near his family's home. At twenty-five, Francesco and his new wife Barbara moved to New York City, where he worked at Caffè Bondì, Ciao Europa, Vivolo, Letizia, and Il Bagatto. But it was when he met Mario Massa, a Ligurian restaurateur with a passion for the food of the Val d'Aosta, that Francesco put the cuisine of yet another Italian region under his belt: the two men opened La Grolla together in 1998, and it is there that Francesco offers patrons classic Valdostano dishes like rigatoni with melting Fontina sauce and tagliatelle with mushrooms.

bucatini with sardines and fennel A sunny Sicilian pasta featuring fresh sardines.

Trim the fennel bulbs: remove the tough outer layer, cut them in quarters, core them, and julienne them. Sauté the julienned fennel in a large sauté pan with the olive oil and garlic for 5 minutes over medium heat; stir in the tomatoes and parsley, and cook for 5 more minutes. Pour in 1 cup of water, lower the heat to medium-low, and cook for another 20 minutes, adding more water if the liquid in the pan dries out. Season with salt and pepper.

Meanwhile, toast the bread crumbs in a hot skillet, stirring them to brown them evenly; the bread crumbs are done when the color changes to a light golden brown and they smell faintly nutty. Set aside.

Bring 5 quarts of water to a boil, and add the bucatini and salt; 5 minutes before the bucatini are cooked (about 4 minutes after you drop them into the boiling water), fold the sardines into the fennel sauce in the pan.

Drain the bucatini, toss them with the sauce in the pan, and turn out onto a serving platter. Top the bucatini with the toasted bread crumbs, and serve hot.

serves 4

3 fennel bulbs
3 tablespoons extra-virgin olive oil
3 garlic cloves, minced
10 plum tomatoes, cubed
2 tablespoons minced Italian parsley
salt and freshly ground black pepper
3 tablespoons fresh bread crumbs
1 pound bucatini
20 fresh sardines, gutted, deboned,
   and rinsed

springtime orecchini You can
use cavatelli instead of orecchini for this refreshing dish. Be sure to select firm, unblemished fava beans, and slip off the skin on each bean after blanching.

serves 4

2 pounds fresh fava beans, shelled
2 pounds baby artichokes
I lemon, halved
4 garlic cloves, minced
3 tablespoons extra-virgin olive oil
I pound frozen or shelled fresh peas
salt and freshly ground black pepper
I bunch Italian parsley, leaves only,
    minced
I pound orecchini
10 mint leaves
juice of 2 lemons

Shell the fava beans and cook them in 5 quarts of boiling water for 2 minutes; remove with a slotted spoon to a bowl of cold water and slip off the skins. Set aside, reserving the water. (If you have a pasta insert, use it: it will make draining the fava beans much simpler.)

Trim the artichokes, removing the tough outer leaves and scooping out the hairy inner choke from each one; immediately rub each artichoke with the cut lemon, slice each artichoke in fine strips, and drop into a bowl of water acidulated with the juice from the halved lemon.

In a pan large enough to accommodate the orecchini later, cook the garlic in the olive oil for 30 seconds over medium heat; add the fava beans, the artichoke slices, the peas, and 1/3 cup of water; cook for 5 minutes. Season with salt and pepper, add the parsley, and cook for 15 more minutes.

Meanwhile, add the orecchini and salt to the reserved boiling water, and cook until al dente; drain. Toss the orecchini with the vegetable sauce, the mint leaves, and the lemon juice, and serve immediately.

pappardelle with porcini, chicken livers, and tomatoes

Typical country fare in Tuscany. Substitute veal if you are not fond of chicken livers.

In a sauté pan large enough to accommodate the pappardelle later, sauté the chicken livers in the olive oil until evenly browned, about 10 minutes over medium heat. Add the garlic and onion, and cook for 3 minutes. Stir in the flour; cook for 30 seconds to get rid of the raw taste of the flour. Deglaze with the wine, and when it evaporates, add the porcini, tomatoes, parsley, salt, pepper, and 1 cup of water; bring to a boil and cook for 20 minutes over low heat.

Meanwhile, bring 5 quarts of water to a boil. Cook the pappardelle with salt until al dente; drain. Toss the pappardelle with the sauce in the pan, adjust the seasoning if needed, and serve hot.

serves 6

2 pounds chicken livers, cubed
$^{1}/_{4}$ cup extra-virgin olive oil
2 garlic cloves, minced
$^{1}/_{2}$ white onion, diced
$^{1}/_{2}$ cup flour
$^{2}/_{3}$ cup dry white wine
1 pound porcini mushrooms,
   scrubbed and diced
10 plum tomatoes, diced
1 bunch Italian parsley, leaves only,
   minced
salt and freshly ground black pepper
1 pound pappardelle

pasta e fagioli alla napoletana

Francesco was born near Naples, on the Amalfi Coast, and this hearty bean and pasta dish reminds him of the flavors of home.

serves 8

For the soup:
$1/2$ white onion, minced
2 garlic cloves, minced
$1/2$ cup extra-virgin olive oil
2 pounds dry cannellini beans,
    soaked in water to cover for 24 hours
    and drained
2 celery hearts, sliced
6 plum tomatoes, chopped
10 basil leaves, torn
8 ounces mezzi tubetti
salt and freshly ground black pepper
For the infused oil:
$1/2$ cup extra-virgin olive oil
8 rosemary sprigs
16 sage leaves
3 garlic cloves, crushed
1 fresh chili pepper

Make the soup: In a pot, sauté the onion and garlic in the olive oil for 5 minutes over medium heat. Add the cannellini beans and 4 quarts of water, bring to a gentle boil, lower the heat to medium-low, and cook for $1\frac{1}{2}$ hours, or until the beans are tender, adding more water if necessary to keep the beans covered.

Meanwhile, make the infused oil: Heat the olive oil with the rosemary, sage, garlic, and chili pepper for 5 minutes over medium-low heat, or until the oil becomes aromatic; strain and set aside.

When the beans are cooked, add the celery hearts, tomatoes, basil, and mezzi tubetti to the pot; cook until the mezzi tubetti are done, about 10 minutes. Add salt and pepper, and ladle into 8 soup bowls. Drizzle each serving with the infused olive oil, and serve immediately.

rigatoni with creamy fontina

sauce Perfect for a winter's night, this dish is typical of Val d'Aosta, a region located almost entirely in the Northwestern Italian Alps. Francesco suggests topping each serving with a pyramid of shaved white truffles.

In a 3-quart pot, melt the butter over medium heat and whisk in the flour. Cook, stirring, for 3 minutes; pour in the heavy cream and milk, whisking all the while to avoid lumps, and bring to a boil. Lower the heat and simmer for 10 minutes, or until the sauce resembles a velvety cream. Fold the Fontina into the cream mixture, stir until melted, add the egg yolks, and whisk rapidly so the yolks do not scramble. Season with salt and pepper, and fold in the parsley; set aside.

Bring 5 quarts of water to a boil, and add the rigatoni and salt; cook until al dente, and drain. Return to the pot, fold in the Fontina sauce and Parmigiano, and spoon into 4 heated bowls. Top with the truffles and serve immediately.

serves 4

2 sticks (16 tablespoons) unsalted butter
1 cup flour
1 quart heavy cream, heated
2 cups whole milk, heated
$^1/_2$ pound Fontina from Val d'Aosta, cubed
2 egg yolks
salt and freshly ground black pepper
$^1/_2$ bunch Italian parsley, leaves only, minced
1 pound rigatoni
$^1/_2$ cup freshly grated Parmigiano Reggiano
1 white truffle, shaved (optional)

don
curtiss

zite with sausage, pine nuts, currants, and arugula • scampi- and porcini-laced fettuccine • spaghettini with mussels and sausage • cavatelli and venison ragù • creamy farfalle with mushrooms and asparagus

Rocky Salskov

Looking back on his seventeen-year successful run in the restaurant business, one would never guess that Don Curtiss, Executive Chef of Seattle's Prego Ristorante, hadn't planned a career in the kitchen: he was studying accounting and finance at the University of Minnesota when his part-time job as Sous Chef at a local restaurant moved him to trade his calculator for a double boiler. Born and raised in Minnesota, Don began his Northwest culinary adventure in 1994 as Executive Chef at Al Boccalino, then went on to Andaluca Restaurant. He soon took the helm of the kitchen at Assaggio, and in 1999, he became Executive Chef at the newly renovated, elegant Prego Ristorante. "I designed the menu at Prego to reflect my preference for native ingredients like wild sturgeon and Dungeness crabs. The dishes I offer underscore the interplay between the Northwest and Italy: local foods marrying with thousands of years of Italian tradition. I look at what's fresh at the market that day, then set out to create the specials." Typical pastas at Prego include linguine with a medley of fresh fish and seafood, ravioli in Dungeness crab sauce and spicy tomato broth, and capellini tossed with just-harvested mushrooms and herbs from Don's herb garden out back. And, true to local flavors, Don meets the Northwestern predilection for game cookery with robust wild boar dishes and a heavenly offering of cavatelli in venison ragù.

zite with sausage, pine nuts, currants, and arugula A Sicilian-inspired

dish Don developed to draw the most flavor from saffron. The slightly pungent arugula he folds in at the end blends perfectly with the sweetness of the currants.

Heat the broth in a small saucepan. Dissolve the saffron in it; set aside.

In a 12" sauté pan, melt the butter. Add the sausage and cook until lightly browned all over, about 10 minutes over medium heat, stirring often to cook evenly. Stir in the pine nuts and sauté for 1 minute, or until the pine nuts take on a pretty golden color. Fold in the currants, salt, pepper, and saffron-infused broth. Reduce by half over medium-high heat, about 5 minutes; stir in the cream and cook until fairly thick, about 5 more minutes.

While the sauce is reducing, bring 5 quarts of water to a boil. Add the zite and salt, and cook until al dente. Drain the zite and toss in a heated serving bowl with $1/4$ cup of the Pecorino, the baby arugula, and enough sauce to coat the pasta; the sauce should be barely clinging to the pasta. Sprinkle with the remaining Pecorino and the parsley, and serve, passing the remaining sauce at the table.

serves 4

1 cup chicken broth (see page 183)
$1/2$ teaspoon saffron
2 tablespoons unsalted butter
1 pound spicy Italian sausage,
    casings removed and crumbled
$1/4$ cup pine nuts
$1/4$ cup currants
salt and freshly ground black pepper
$1 1/2$ cups heavy cream
1 pound zite
$1/3$ cup freshly grated Pecorino Romano
$1/2$ cup baby arugula, washed,
    stems removed
2 tablespoons chopped Italian parsley

scampi- and porcini-laced
fettuccine
The ultimate luxury: scampi, porcini, and cream are tossed with fettuccine for a spectacular first course.

Preheat the broiler: Line a baking sheet with aluminum foil and place the pepper on it; broil until blistered on all sides and blackened all over, turning 3 times, for about 20 minutes. Remove from the oven, wrap in the aluminum foil, and cool to room temperature. Unwrap, peel, seed, and dice the roasted pepper. Set aside.

In a 12" sauté pan, melt the butter. Add the scallion, roasted pepper, porcini, salt, and pepper. Sauté until the scallion is translucent and the porcini are cooked, about 10 minutes over medium heat. Pour in the Prosecco, broth, tomato sauce, and cream. Raise the heat to medium-high and reduce by half, about 5 minutes. Fold in the shelled scampi tails and the halved scampi. Cook over medium heat until the scampi are cooked and the sauce is sufficiently reduced to cling to the pasta, about 5 minutes.

While the sauce is reducing, bring 5 quarts of water to a boil. Add the fettuccine and salt, and cook until al dente. Drain.

Remove the scampi halves from the sauce and set aside. Toss the fettuccine with the sauce in the skillet, fold in half of the chives, adjust the salt if needed, and transfer to a warm terra-cotta serving bowl.

Arrange the scampi halves so that the claws hang slightly over the rim of the bowl, and sprinkle the fettuccine with the remaining chives. Serve immediately.

serves 4

1 red pepper
2 tablespoons unsalted butter
1 scallion, sliced
4 porcini mushrooms,
    scrubbed and sliced
salt and freshly ground black pepper
1/4 cup Prosecco
1/2 cup fish broth (see page 184)
1 1/2 cups tomato sauce (see page 185)
3/4 cup heavy cream
1 pound shelled scampi tails
4 whole scampi, cut in half lengthwise
1 pound fettuccine
1 tablespoon snipped chives

spaghettini with mussels and sausage
An unusual combination of seafood and meat that Don particularly enjoys when he needs a boost of energy. Use sausage laced with fennel seeds if you like a subtle anise flavor.

Scrub the mussels and remove any beards with a paring knife. Place in a bowl, cover with cold water, and add 1 tablespoon of salt; set aside to soak for 30 minutes, then drain and rinse.

Heat a 12" skillet and add the olive oil, garlic, salt, pepper, and chili flakes; cook over medium heat until the garlic starts to turn golden, about 30 seconds. Stir in the sausage and cook until it is lightly browned all over, stirring often, about 8 minutes. Add the mussels and cook for 2 minutes, or until the mussels start to open. Pour in the wine, broth, and tomato sauce. Cook until the mussels are all open and the sauce is reduced, about 5 minutes. This sauce can be a little brothy if you prefer, or you can reduce it longer so that it clings to the pasta.

While the sauce is reducing, bring 5 quarts of water to a boil; add the spaghettini and salt, and cook until al dente; drain. Toss the spaghettini in the skillet with the sauce, and fold in half of the parsley.

Transfer the spaghettini to a terra-cotta bowl, arranging the mussels around the outside rim. Sprinkle the remaining parsley over the top and serve immediately.

serves 6

2 pounds mussels
salt
1 tablespoon extra-virgin olive oil
3 garlic cloves, coarsely chopped
freshly ground black pepper
$1/8$ teaspoon chili flakes
salt
8 ounces Italian sausage,
  casings removed and crumbled
$1/2$ cup dry white wine
1 cup fish broth (see page 184)
1 cup tomato sauce (see page 185)
1 pound spaghettini
1 tablespoon chopped Italian parsley

cavatelli and venison

ragù Barolo and Marsala combine with rosemary, sage, cinnamon, and nutmeg to give the venison ragù its distinct character.

serves 4

2 tablespoons extra-virgin olive oil
2 pounds ground venison
salt and freshly ground black pepper
1 tablespoon chopped rosemary
1 tablespoon chopped sage
1 onion, diced
$1/2$ teaspoon ground cinnamon
$1/4$ teaspoon freshly grated nutmeg
$1/2$ cup Marsala
$1/2$ cup Barolo
$1/4$ cup balsamic vinegar
1 cup chicken broth (see page 183)
4 cups canned strained plum tomatoes
1 pound cavatelli
$1/4$ cup freshly grated Parmigiano
   Reggiano
$1/4$ cup shaved Parmigiano Reggiano
1 tablespoon chopped Italian parsley

In an 8-quart saucepan, heat the olive oil until it is smoking. Add the venison and cook, stirring often over medium heat, until it browns evenly, about 5 minutes. Stir in the salt, pepper, rosemary, sage, onion, cinnamon, and nutmeg, and continue to cook until the onion is translucent and the venison is fully cooked, about 5 minutes. Pour in the Marsala, Barolo, vinegar, broth, and tomatoes, and simmer for 2 to 2$1/2$ hours, or until the ragù is fairly thick, stirring once in a while.

Meanwhile, bring 5 quarts of water to a boil. Add the cavatelli and salt, and cook until al dente; drain, and return to the pot. Stir in half of the ragù and fold in the grated Parmigiano. Transfer to a warm terra-cotta serving bowl. Mound the shaved Parmigiano in the center of the pasta. Sprinkle with the parsley and serve immediately, passing the remaining ragù at the table.

creamy **farfalle** with mushrooms and asparagus

Don sometimes substitutes Speck (a smoked ham from Trentino-Alto Adige) for the smoked chicken in the sauce for an Alpine flavor.

Bring 6 quarts of water to a boil. Add the asparagus and salt, and cook for 2 minutes; remove with a slotted spoon to a bowl of cold water to stop the cooking and set the color. Drain and cut into 1" pieces. Reserve the pot of boiling water.

Trim the artichokes, removing the tough outer leaves and scooping out the hairy inner choke. Quarter each artichoke and place in a bowl of cold water with the lemon juice to prevent the artichokes from turning black.

In a 12" skillet, melt the butter. Add the smoked chicken, the drained artichokes, the asparagus, mushrooms, salt, and pepper. Sauté over medium heat for 3 minutes, or until the mushrooms are starting to soften. Pour in the Marsala and broth, bring to a boil, and reduce by half. Stir in the tomato sauce and cream, and cook until the sauce is fairly thick, about 10 minutes.

While the sauce is reducing, return the water to a boil. Add the farfalle and cook until al dente; drain. Toss in the skillet with the sauce, and fold in the grated Parmigiano. Make sure the sauce is clinging to the pasta and is not too liquid; if you need to, reduce it a little over medium-high heat.

Transfer to a warm terra-cotta serving bowl. Mound the shaved Parmigiano in the center of the bowl, and sprinkle with the parsley. Serve immediately.

serves 4

4 pencil-thin asparagus spears, trimmed
salt
2 artichokes
juice of 1 lemon
2 tablespoons unsalted butter
3 ounces smoked chicken, diced
4 cremini mushrooms,
    scrubbed and sliced
freshly ground black pepper
$1/4$ cup Marsala
$1/4$ cup chicken broth (see page 183)
$1 1/2$ cups tomato sauce (see page 185)
$1/2$ cup heavy cream
1 pound farfalle
$1/3$ cup freshly grated Parmigiano Reggiano
$1/4$ cup shaved Parmigiano Reggiano
1 tablespoon chopped Italian parsley

luigi
diotaiuti

linguine in lobster sauce • sedani con
la norma • gnocchi with sausage • baked
lamb and eggplant rigatoni • smoked
mozzarella-asparagus penne

When Luigi Diotaiuti had to pick a name for his restaurant in Washington, D.C. back in 1996, it didn't take him long to come up with something he liked: Al Tiramisu was born in a flash of inspiration. "I wanted people to come to my place and find fun, joy, and good cheer. That's what tiramisu means: it means cheer me up. And it's also one of my most famous desserts," he explains. True to his restaurant's name, Luigi offers fun, joy, and good cheer to anyone who comes through his door. A native of Basilicata, Luigi lived in Tuscany and honed his culinary skills in Italy and, later, in Paris. After moving to Washington in 1990 and working in some of its best Italian restaurants—Donna Adele, Primi Piatti, and Duca di Milano—he opened his own place. Today, he is hailed as one of D.C.'s top chefs. Regulars flock to his restaurant for a taste of Luigi's fish carpaccios, his exuberant pastas, and his dramatic desserts, which include far more than just tiramisu. And since Luigi is a man with energy to spare, he spends Saturdays in his restaurant's kitchen, teaching hands-on cooking classes. Not surprisingly, one of his favorite subjects is pasta: "I love to get my hands in the dough, and to show people that it's not so complicated. It's all about passion, about letting your instincts guide you."

linguine in lobster sauce This luxurious
lobster dish is a favorite at Al Tiramisu. "The real trick here is to not overcook the lobster, or it will become rubbery," says Luigi. Look for small lobsters for better flavor: they tend to be sweeter than their larger counterparts.

Bring 6 quarts of water to a boil. Add the lemon, onion, bay leaves, wine, and salt; cook 5 minutes to develop the flavors. Drop in the lobster. Cook for 7 minutes, drain, and cool to room temperature. Remove the lobster meat carefully from the shell, saving the head, tail, and claw shells for the final presentation. When the lobster meat is cool, cut it into bite-size pieces.

In a saucepan, heat 2 tablespoons of the olive oil and add the garlic. Cook until aromatic, about 30 seconds; fold in the lobster meat, and cook 1 minute. Deglaze the pan with the cognac or brandy and let it reduce by half. Add the tomato sauce and 1 tablespoon of the parsley. Cook over medium heat for 5 minutes.

Meanwhile, bring 5 quarts of water to a boil; add the linguine and salt, and cook until the linguine are al dente; drain, and toss into the pan with the lobster sauce. Sauté over high heat for 1 minute to mingle the flavors.

To serve, spoon the linguine onto the center of a large serving plate. Place the lobster head at one end, the tail at the other, and the two claws on either side of its head. Drizzle with the remaining olive oil, sprinkle with the pepper, and garnish with the remaining parsley. Serve hot.

serves 4

$1/_2$ lemon
$1/_2$ onion
5 bay leaves
1 cup dry white wine
salt
one 1-pound lobster
$1/_4$ cup extra-virgin olive oil
2 garlic cloves, minced
$1/_4$ cup cognac or brandy
$1/_2$ cup tomato sauce (see page 185)
2 tablespoons minced Italian parsley
1 pound linguine
freshly ground black pepper

sedani con la norma
Sicily's famous eggplant-topped pasta—named after Vincenzo Bellini's heroine, Norma—is simple to prepare and especially lovely in the summer, when eggplants are in season. Luigi's version is lighter, and calls for sautéing cubed eggplant rather than frying sliced eggplant.

serves 4

3 tablespoons extra-virgin olive oil
1 onion, chopped
2 garlic cloves, minced
1 eggplant, peeled and cut into $1/2$" cubes
2 cups canned chopped plum tomatoes
salt and freshly ground black pepper
1 pound sedani
$1/3$ cup freshly grated ricotta salata

In a pan large enough to accommodate the sedani later, heat the olive oil and sauté the onion and garlic until softened, about 3 minutes over medium heat; stir in the eggplant cubes, and cook for 5 minutes. Add the tomatoes and cook for 15 minutes longer. Season with salt and pepper.

Meanwhile, bring 5 quarts of water to a boil, drop in the sedani and salt, and cook until the sedani are al dente. Drain.

Toss the sedani into the sauce. Sprinkle with half of the ricotta, stir gently, and transfer to a serving platter. Top with the remaining ricotta, and serve hot.

gnocchi with sausage
Luigi admits to a
fondness for strong, decided flavors, so he adds 1 teaspoon of chili flakes to the
sauce to give it a chili kick. If you like, you can serve conchiglie, rigatoni,
or even mezze zite with this chunky sausage sauce: each of these pasta shapes is
ideal for catching the bits of sausage. Avoid egg pastas like tagliatelle, which would
be overwhelmed by the intensity of the flavors.

Heat the olive oil in a saucepan. Add the garlic and cook for 30 seconds, or until
aromatic, watching that the garlic doesn't burn. As soon as the garlic starts changing
color and becoming golden, add the sausage and cook until it is evenly browned, stirring often. Add the tomato sauce and cook the sauce over medium heat for 15 to 20
minutes, stirring once in a while.

   Meanwhile, bring 5 quarts of water to a boil. Add the gnocchi and salt, and cook
until al dente. Drain the gnocchi, return to the pot, and fold in the sauce; cook for 1
minute to mingle the flavors, adjusting the salt if needed. Transfer to a pretty serving
platter, top with the parsley and Pecorino, and serve hot.

serves 4

1/4 cup extra-virgin olive oil
1 garlic clove, minced
12 ounces Italian sausage,
   casings removed and crumbled
2 cups tomato sauce (see page 185)
1 pound dried gnocchi
salt
2 tablespoons minced Italian parsley
1/4 cup freshly grated Pecorino Sardo

baked lamb and eggplant

rigatoni Pairing lamb and eggplant is traditional in the Mediterranean, and is especially prevalent in Southern Italy, where gorgeous eggplants are cultivated and succulent, milk-fed lamb is a favored meat. Luigi serves this elegant dish cut into wedges and accompanied by a refreshing tomato sauce.

Cut the lamb into $1/2$" cubes, removing all traces of fat and sinew. Heat 2 tablespoons of the olive oil in a pan; add half of the onion and all of the rosemary and thyme. Cook over medium heat until the onion has browned lightly, about 5 minutes; add the lamb, and stir to brown evenly. After 5 minutes, pour in the wine and allow it to evaporate before adding the tomato sauce. Cook over low heat until the sauce is somewhat reduced and the lamb is done, about 20 minutes.

Cook the eggplant slices in 1 quart of boiling water for 3 minutes; drain and cool. Set aside as many slices as needed to cover the bottom and sides of an 8" ovenproof mold, and dice the rest of the eggplant into $1/2$" pieces.

Heat the remaining olive oil and sauté the diced eggplant with the remaining onion for 5 minutes, or until the eggplant is soft; set aside.

Preheat the oven to 325°. Bring 5 quarts of water to a boil. Add the rigatoni and salt, and cook until al dente; drain. Set aside as many rigatoni as you will need to form a ring around the mold; toss the remaining rigatoni in a bowl with the lamb sauce, the sautéed eggplant, besciamella, basil, and Fontina. Stir to combine.

Line the bottom and sides of a well-buttered mold with the rigatoni and eggplant slices, and fill the middle with the pasta mixture. Bake for 20 minutes; carefully invert the mold onto a serving platter, let it rest for 5 minutes, and then remove the mold gently to release the pasta. Serve hot.

serves 6

12 ounces lamb
3 tablespoons extra-virgin olive oil
1 onion, minced
2 rosemary sprigs, leaves only, minced
2 thyme sprigs, leaves only, minced
1 cup dry red wine
1 cup tomato sauce (see page 185)
3 eggplants, peeled and sliced
1 pound rigatoni
salt
2 cups besciamella (see page 185)
6 basil leaves, torn
8 ounces Fontina from Val d'Aosta, cubed
2 tablespoons unsalted butter

smoked mozzarella-asparagus

penne Look for firm, unblemished, pencil-thin asparagus, and discard the woody ends; reserve the pretty tips as a garnish.

Bring 5 quarts of water to a boil. Drop in the asparagus, and cook for 2 minutes; remove with a slotted spoon to a bowl of ice water, drain, and cut into 1" pieces, reserving the tips as a garnish. Reserve the pot of boiling water.

Heat the olive oil in a saucepan. Add the garlic and cook until golden, about 30 seconds over medium-high heat. Remove the garlic from the pan, and add the tomatoes and salt. Sauté for 2 minutes, still over medium-high heat. Fold in the asparagus (minus the tips) and immediately remove from the heat. Set aside.

Drop the penne rigate and salt into the reserved boiling water, and cook until al dente; drain. Toss the penne rigate with the sauce in the pan, fold in the mozzarella, basil, and Parmigiano, and adjust the seasoning if needed. Serve immediately, garnished with the asparagus tips.

serves 4

24 pencil-thin asparagus spears, trimmed
1/4 cup extra-virgin olive oil
1 garlic clove, crushed
6 San Marzano
   or 12 cherry tomatoes, diced
salt
1 pound spinach penne rigate
12 ounces smoked mozzarella, cubed
1 bunch basil, leaves only, torn
1/4 cup freshly grated Parmigiano
   Reggiano

Greg Klim

charles **draghi**

strozzapreti in bagna cauda •

farfalle with walnuts and oregano •

orecchiette with speck and

marjoram • tagliatelle with roasted

beets and mint • pappardelle with

wilted arugula and scallion greens

Charles Draghi—Chuck to family and friends—will tell you that it all started when his uncle Eddy purchased the complete furnishings of an old-style Wurlitzer diner and set up a private restaurant for his family in the foreman's shed of an old tobacco barn in Connecticut. "My uncle hunted pheasant and venison and made it into a ragù to serve over polenta, and he made the best risotto you ever tasted," he recalls. Spurred on by an early passion for cooking and a family who viewed fine food as a necessity rather than a luxury, Charles became Executive Chef of Marcuccio's in Boston's North End after stints in a number of the nation's top restaurants, including Restaurant Jean Claude in SoHo, L'Americain in Hartford, Connecticut, and Restaurant 28 in Monclair, New Jersey. "I don't use any butter or cream in my sauces. Olive oil is it for me. And I rely on the natural roasting pan juices to get the necessary viscosity for a good sauce," he says. As a result of his inventive techniques and meticulous choice of ingredients—nothing less than perfect will do—his clientele is now hooked on Charles' Italian food and his impressive all-Italian varietal wine list. Charles' signature dishes include strozzapreti in a creamy anchovy-laced roasted pepper sauce, fusilli with roasted corn, yellow peppers, tomatoes, and rosemary, steamed razor clams with Tocai wine and fennel seeds, and wild boar in fruit must. "I want my customers to feel something when they taste my food. The worst thing is to leave people indifferent, as far I'm concerned."

strozzapreti in bagna cauda

Bagna cauda is a garlicky, anchovy-based Piedmontese sauce, traditionally used for dipping raw and cooked vegetables and often poured over a plate of roasted peppers as an antipasto.

serves 4

4 red peppers
1 head garlic
2 cups pine nuts
12 anchovy filets
$^1\!/_4$ cup capers
8 sage leaves
2 cups extra-virgin olive oil
24 pencil-thin asparagus spears, trimmed and cut into 2" lengths
1 pound strozzapreti
salt
$^1\!/_4$ cup freshly grated Parmigiano Reggiano

Preheat the broiler: Line a baking sheet with aluminum foil and place the peppers on it; broil until blistered and blackened, turning 3 times, for about 20 minutes. Remove from the oven, wrap in the foil, and cool. Unwrap, peel, seed, and slice the peppers. Set aside. Lower the oven to 450° and roast the head of garlic, wrapping it in aluminum foil first, for 45 minutes; squeeze the cloves out of the skins. Lower the oven to 375°. Place the pine nuts on a baking sheet; bake for 10 minutes, or until golden. In a food processor, blend the anchovies, roasted peppers, garlic, 1 cup of the pine nuts, the capers, sage, and 1 cup of the olive oil until smooth; this is the sauce.

Meanwhile, bring 5 quarts of water to a boil. Drop in the asparagus and cook for 2 minutes; remove with a slotted spoon to a bowl of cold water. Add the strozzapreti and salt to the boiling water, and cook until al dente. Drain. Toss the strozzapreti with the remaining olive oil, the remaining pine nuts, and the asparagus. Spoon into 4 heated bowls, top with the sauce, and garnish with the Parmigiano. Serve hot.

farfalle with walnuts and oregano

Charles' cooking style relies on an ingenious use of herbs to underscore the character of other components in each dish.

Bring 5 quarts of water to a boil and add the farfalle and salt; cook until al dente and drain, reserving 2 cups of the pasta cooking water.

Meanwhile, in a sauté pan large enough to accommodate the farfalle later, heat 2 tablespoons of the olive oil over medium heat. Add all but 2 tablespoons of the walnuts and toast them, shaking the pan back and forth often, until the perfume of the walnuts rises, about 3 minutes. Add $1/8$ teaspoon of the pepper, and turn down the heat to medium-low.

Stir in the tomatoes, then the oregano, and sauté for 1 minute; add the saffron, the reserved pasta cooking water, and the remaining olive oil, and turn off the heat under the pan. Allow the mixture in the pan to sit for 3 minutes, then add the farfalle. Toss to coat the farfalle with the sauce, and spoon into 4 heated plates. Top with the remaining pepper and walnuts, and sprinkle with the Parmigiano. Serve hot.

serves 4

1 pound farfalle
salt
1 cup extra-virgin olive oil
2 cups shelled walnuts
$1/4$ teaspoon cracked black pepper
4 large heirloom tomatoes, diced
4 oregano sprigs, leaves only, minced
$1/2$ teaspoon saffron
$1/2$ cup freshly grated Parmigiano
    Reggiano

orecchiette with speck and marjoram

Charles uses Speck, a fragrant smoked ham from Northern Italy, to lend a meaty flavor to the orecchiette.

Bring 6 quarts of water to a boil in a pot with a pasta insert, and add the peas; cook until tender, about 5 minutes, then remove the pasta insert and drain the peas; reserve the cooking water and keep it boiling.

Separate the fat from the meat in the Speck, and dice each separately. In a sauté pan, render the fat of the Speck over medium heat until translucent, about 2 minutes, then add the potato and cook until tender, about 10 minutes.

Meanwhile, cook the orecchiette with salt until al dente in the reserved boiling water, then drain, reserving 1 cup of the pasta cooking water.

Add the orecchiette to the potato in the pan, along with the diced meat of the Speck, all but 2 tablespoons of the olive oil, the peas, marjoram, half of the parsley, and the cracked black pepper. Pour in enough of the reserved pasta cooking water to dilute the sauce as necessary.

Toss to combine, adjust the salt if needed, and spoon into 4 heated bowls. Garnish with the remaining olive oil and parsley, and top with the Parmigiano. Serve hot.

serves 4

2 cups shelled fresh peas
one 1-pound slice of Speck,
  fat still attached
1 large potato, peeled
  and cut into $1/4$" cubes
1 pound orecchiette
salt
1 cup extra-virgin olive oil
1 teaspoon minced marjoram
1 tablespoon minced Italian parsley
$1/4$ teaspoon cracked black pepper
$1/4$ cup freshly grated Parmigiano
  Reggiano

tagliatelle with roasted beets and mint

The smoky sweetness of roasted beets and the vibrant aroma of fresh mint combine with Prosciutto in a simple and delightful pasta sauce.

serves 4

2 pounds beets, leaves still attached
4 ounces Prosciutto, thinly sliced
1 cup extra-virgin olive oil
$1/4$ teaspoon cracked black pepper
1 pound tagliatelle
salt
1 bunch mint, leaves only
$1/2$ cup freshly grated Parmigiano
   Reggiano

Preheat the oven to 400°. Wash the beets and greens. Separate the greens from the beet roots. Place the beet roots in a baking dish, and bake until tender and blackened, about 1 hour. Cool, then slip off the skins and julienne, saving any roasting juices.

Remove the fatty strips from the Prosciutto, and sauté over medium heat in $1/2$ cup of the olive oil until translucent, about 3 minutes; reserve the meaty part of the Prosciutto and cut it into strips. Add half of the cracked black pepper, the julienned beets, and the beet greens to the pan, and cook for 2 minutes, or until the leaves wilt.

Meanwhile, bring 5 quarts of water to a boil. Add the tagliatelle and salt, and cook until al dente. Drain, reserving 1 cup of the pasta cooking water. Toss the tagliatelle in the pan with the sauce, the remaining olive oil, all but 2 of the mint sprigs, enough of the reserved pasta cooking water to dilute the sauce, and the Parmigiano. Serve hot, topped with the reserved mint, cracked pepper, and strips of Prosciutto.

pappardelle with wilted arugula and scallion greens

Easy enough to make on a busy weeknight, this pasta sauce requires no cooking: just combine a half dozen flavorful ingredients in a bowl, and toss with the pasta to create a mouthwatering first course.

Bring 5 quarts of water to a boil and add the pappardelle and salt; cook until al dente and drain, reserving I cup of the pasta cooking water.

Meanwhile, place the arugula, scallion greens, and basil leaves in a large serving bowl. Add the lemon zest, nutmeg, and ¼ cup of the Parmigiano.

Pour the reserved pasta cooking water into the bowl, and let the heat slightly wilt the arugula and scallions and melt the Parmigiano, stirring with a rubber spatula. Stir in the olive oil, along with the pappardelle, and toss thoroughly. Garnish with the remaining Parmigiano and the pepper, and serve hot.

serves 4

I pound pappardelle
salt
I bunch arugula, washed, stems removed, and torn
6 scallions, green part only, minced
I bunch basil, leaves only, torn
grated zest of 2 lemons
¹/₂ teaspoon freshly grated nutmeg
¹/₂ cup freshly grated Parmigiano Reggiano
¹/₂ cup extra-virgin olive oil
¹/₈ teaspoon freshly ground black pepper

efisio &
francesco
farris

sardinian lobster bucatini • clam and fregola soup • malloreddus in wild boar ragù • rigatoni with ricotta and bottarga • gnocchetti sardi and seafood medley

Families that eat together stay together—that's the old Italian adage. Brothers Efisio (left) and Francesco Farris (right) have put a new spin on this bit of wisdom. Their motto: Families that work together stay together. Co-owners, with Efisio's wife Lori, of three hugely successful Sardinian restaurants in Texas (Arcodoro and Pomodoro in Dallas, and Arcodoro in Houston), Efisio and Francesco know that the key to success is to never lose sight of your roots. "When we first came to the States from Sardinia, we offered varied Italian fare: Tuscan and Piedmontese dishes, things our Texan clientele was familiar with. But as we grew more popular, we become more daring in our approach, and we changed the menu to incorporate the foods that we had grown up eating back in Sardinia," explains Efisio, who obtained a degree in design and architecture in Rome before making the big move to America and changing careers to follow his love for cooking. The response to Efisio and Francesco's bold new style of regional Sardinian cuisine was enthusiastic. Critics hailed their restaurants as havens of Sardinian hospitality. The brothers introduced Americans to previously unknown ingredients like myrtle, pane carasau, and fregola, all Sardinian staples that find creative use in the Farris' kitchen. Among their top-selling dishes: fregola and cockle soup, tiny Sardinian gnocchi with seafood ragù or braised wild boar, roasted lamb with fennel, puffy pillows of dough stuffed with sweetened ricotta and bathed in bitter honey. "Our clients know that they can find fettuccine Alfredo elsewhere. What they want from us is a taste of Sardinia, and that's what we deliver," says Francesco, just as proud as his older brother Efisio of bringing the flavors and traditions of his beloved island to American soil.

sardinian lobster **bucatini**

Efisio and Francesco suggest you use a Vernaccia Secca di Oristano or Malvasia Secca di Bosa in the sauce for this traditional Sardinian pasta. Efisio also points out that to better preserve the flavor and fragrance of the lobsters, they should be cut while still alive and cooked immediately thereafter; since that might prove difficult for most home cooks, you can ask the fishmonger to kill the lobsters for you.

Cut the whole lobsters (including the shell) into medallions and set aside.

In a sauté pan, combine the tomatoes, broth, and $1/2$ cup of the wine. Bring to a gentle boil over medium heat and cook for 20 minutes; the sauce will reduce by about half as it cooks down.

In another sauté pan, heat the olive oil over medium heat, add the onion and parsley, and cook until the onion softens, about 5 minutes. Add the lobster medallions, stirring frequently, and cook until they turn bright red. Pour in the remaining wine, and cook for 5 minutes; the wine should evaporate. Fold the tomato sauce into the lobster in the pan, and stir in all but 4 of the basil leaves. Bring the mixture up to a boil, and cook for 10 minutes. Season with salt.

In the meantime, bring 5 quarts of water to a boil and drop in the bucatini and salt; cook until al dente. Fold the bucatini into the lobster sauce and stir thoroughly, adjusting the salt if needed. Divide the bucatini among 6 bowls, garnish with the remaining basil leaves, and serve hot.

serves 6

two 1-pound lobsters
2 tomatoes, peeled, seeded, and thinly sliced
1 cup fish broth (see page 184)
1 cup dry white wine
1 cup extra-virgin olive oil
1 onion, finely chopped
1 tablespoon minced Italian parsley
16 basil leaves
salt
1 pound bucatini

clam and **fregola** soup

Cockles are a good alternative to clams: they have very sweet, delicate flesh, and taste similar to Italy's arselle, the sort of clam variety that would be used to make this soup back in Sardinia, says Efisio.

serves 4

2 pounds littleneck clams or cockles
salt
1/2 cup extra-virgin olive oil
2 garlic cloves, minced
1 bunch Italian parsley,
    leaves only, finely chopped
1/8 teaspoon crushed red pepper
1/8 teaspoon saffron
1 pound fregola
6 Roma tomatoes, diced
grated zest of 1 lemon

Wash the clams or cockles thoroughly under running water, and place them in a bowl; add water to cover and stir in 1 tablespoon of salt. Let soak for 30 minutes, then drain and rinse. Place the clams or cockles in a large pot and set the pot over medium heat; cook until the clams or cockles open, about 10 minutes; discard any unopened clams or cockles. Remove the clams or cockles from the pot, strain the cooking juices left in the pot through a filter-lined sieve, and set aside.

Heat the olive oil in the same pot over medium heat. Add the garlic, parsley, and crushed red pepper, and cook until the garlic is barely golden and the aroma is intense, about 30 seconds. Add the clams or cockles, lower the heat to medium-low, and simmer for 5 more minutes. Add the reserved cooking juices to the pot, along with 2 cups of boiling water. Season with salt (remember that the cooking juices are naturally salty). Add the saffron and bring the mixture to a boil. Pour in the fregola, and cook for 10 minutes, stirring every minute or so. Add the tomatoes, and cook for 10 more minutes; you may need to add some boiling water if the broth dries up too much. The fregola should be cooked by now; cook a little longer if it is not. Remove from the heat and stir in the lemon zest. Adjust the salt if necessary, and serve hot.

malloreddus in wild boar

ragù Sardinians are masters of game cookery; this wild boar ragù is one of their specialties. If possible, buy aged Sardinian Pecorino to sprinkle on the dish.

serves 4

2 tablespoons extra-virgin olive oil
1 garlic clove, peeled
1 shallot, chopped
1 pound top round of wild boar,
  cut into 1/2" cubes
1 cup Cannonau or other dry red wine
2 1/2 cups canned chopped plum
  tomatoes
4 basil leaves, torn
3 bay leaves
1/4 cup juniper berries, crushed
1 pound malloreddus
salt
1 cup freshly grated aged Pecorino Sardo
  or Pecorino Romano

Heat the olive oil in a saucepan. Add the garlic and cook until browned, about 45 seconds over medium heat, then discard. Add the shallot to the oil, and cook for 2 minutes, or until it just wilts. Scatter the wild boar cubes in the pan in a single layer, and cook until browned on both sides, turning once with tongs. Deglaze the pan with the wine, and cook for 3 minutes, or until the wine nearly evaporates. Add the tomatoes, basil, bay leaves, and juniper berries to the pan, bring to a gentle boil, cover, and lower the heat to medium-low; simmer for 30 minutes. The boar should be tender; cook a little longer if it isn't.

Meanwhile, bring 5 quarts of water to a boil. Add the malloreddus and salt, and cook until al dente. Drain, reserving 1/2 cup of the pasta cooking water, and transfer to a serving bowl. Stir in the wild boar sauce and mix for 1 minute; fold in the Pecorino, adjust the salt if needed, discard the bay leaves, and stir in some of the reserved pasta cooking water if necessary to dilute the sauce. Serve hot.

rigatoni with ricotta and bottarga

Sardinia's famed pressed grey mullet roe is called bottarga, and it is usually grated over spaghetti tossed with parsley, olive oil, and bread crumbs. In this unusual dish, the Farris brothers add ricotta and cream to a sauce that also incorporates bottarga, giving the bottarga a more delicate taste.

Bring 5 quarts of water to a boil in a large pot, and cook the rigatoni with salt until they are al dente; drain.

Meanwhile, combine the cream and ricotta in a non-stick pan large enough to accommodate the rigatoni later; cook over medium heat, whisking, until the mixture liquifies, about 3 minutes.

Stir the rigatoni into the ricotta sauce in the pan, and sauté for 2 minutes; season with the freshly ground black pepper.

Slowly incorporate all but 2 tablespoons of the bottarga and all of the parsley into the rigatoni. Transfer to a serving bowl, drizzle with the olive oil, and serve hot, sprinkled with the remaining bottarga.

serves 6

1 pound rigatoni
salt
1 cup heavy cream
1 1/2 cups fresh ricotta
freshly ground black pepper
1/2 cup freshly grated bottarga
2 tablespoons minced Italian parsley
1 tablespoon extra-virgin olive oil

gnocchetti sardi and seafood medley

Francesco prefers to use saffron-tinted malloreddus for this satisfying dish. He also likes Blue Fancy mussels for the ragù, but suggests that you use whichever mussels are freshest at your market.

Wash the mussels thoroughly and pull off any beards with a paring knife. Rinse the clams under running water. Place the mussels and clams in a bowl; add water to cover and stir 2 tablespoons of salt into the water. Let soak for 30 minutes, then drain and rinse. Place the mussels and clams in a large pot and set the pot over medium heat; cook until the mussels and clams open, about 10 minutes; discard any unopened mussels or clams.

Remove the mussels and clams from the pot, strain the cooking juices left in the pot through a filter-lined sieve, and set aside.

Bring 4 quarts of water to a boil and drop in the lobster bodies; cook for 45 minutes. Turn out into a food mill and push through using a stiff spatula; discard the solids and reserve the resulting lobster cream.

In a non-stick pan, heat the olive oil and add the garlic and parsley; cook over medium heat until the garlic softens, about 30 seconds. Add the shrimp and crushed red pepper, and cook, stirring, for 1 minute. Deglaze with the wine and cook for 3 minutes, or until the wine has evaporated slightly. Stir in the tomatoes, and pour in the reserved cooking juices from the mussels and clams along with 1 cup of the reserved lobster cream. Bring to a boil and cook for 15 minutes. Fold in the monkfish and squid ink; cook 10 more minutes, adding more of the lobster cream as needed to keep the sauce moist rather than dry.

In the meantime, bring 5 quarts of water to a boil and add the gnocchetti sardi and salt; cook until al dente, then drain. Fold the gnocchetti sardi into the seafood sauce in the pan, heat for 1 minute, adjust the salt if needed, and distribute among 6 bowls. Garnish each bowl with 3 mussels and 3 clams, and serve hot.

serves 6

18 mussels
18 Manila clams
salt
1 pound lobster bodies (reserve the tail and claws for other dishes)
$1/2$ cup extra-virgin olive oil
4 garlic cloves, minced
1 bunch Italian parsley, leaves only, finely chopped
8 ounces medium shrimp, shelled and deveined, cut into $1/4$" cubes
$1/8$ teaspoon crushed red pepper
1 cup Vermentino di Sardegna or other dry white wine
2 pounds plum tomatoes, cut into $1/4$" cubes
1 pound skinless monkfish, cut into $1/4$" cubes
2 teaspoons squid ink
1 pound gnocchetti sardi

gianni
fassio

spaghetti aglio e olio • scallop and leek conchiglie • gemelli with smoked trout and pink peppercorns • eliche with gorgonzola and radicchio • mezze zite with asparagus, fonduta, and truffled olive oil

"Food runs in the Fassio blood," Gianni Fassio will tell you in his baritone voice. "My grandfather ran the butcher shop, the salumeria, the greengrocer, and the bakery in Isola d'Asti, a small town in Piedmont. You could say he supplied the whole town with food! And my father Piero owned The Blue Fox in San Francisco, where I worked since I was fourteen." Fassio, who was born in San Francisco but grew up in Piedmont, worked as an accountant before making food his profession. After helping to launch Tortola in San Francisco, Fassio bought The Blue Fox and brought it to the forefront of the culinary scene. In 1990, he created Palio d'Asti, where patrons dine on recipes culled from years of gastronomic research in Piedmont. A chain of espresso and sandwich shops in San Francisco called Palio Paninoteca came next. As Ambassador of Asti for the United States, Fassio continues to promote the cuisine and culture of Piedmont in America, introducing his clientele to Piedmontese dishes like pasta with asparagus, Fonduta, and white truffles, penne with smoked trout, beef shoulder braised in Barolo, and bonet, a hazelnut-chocolate pudding he loved as a young boy.

spaghetti aglio e olio This pasta can be
made with basic ingredients found in any kitchen and is very satisfying after a long day at work, when all you really crave is direct flavors and simple preparation. Gianni sometimes adds a few salted anchovies and pitted black olives, both coarsely chopped, to the garlic-chili oil.

Bring 7 quarts of water to a boil and add the spaghetti and salt; cook until al dente, then drain, reserving ¼ cup of the pasta cooking water.

Meanwhile, in a sauté pan large enough to accommodate the spaghetti later, heat the olive oil over medium heat. Add the chili and garlic, and cook until the garlic becomes golden but not brown, about 1 minute.

Toss the spaghetti in the pan with the oil, being careful not to introduce any water. Once the spaghetti and oil have been mixed, add a little of the reserved pasta cooking water; sauté for 1 minute to mingle the flavors and thicken the sauce. Adjust the salt if needed and serve hot, sprinkled with the pepper.

serves 6

20 ounces spaghetti
salt
⅓ cup extra-virgin olive oil
3 dried chili peppers, crumbled
6 garlic cloves, thinly sliced
freshly ground black pepper

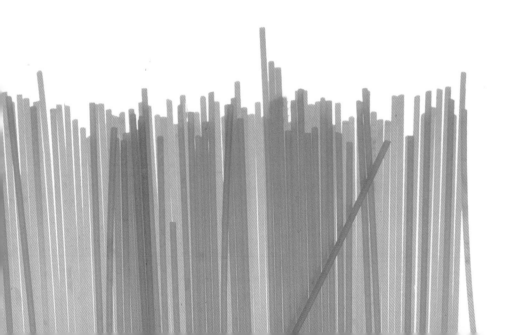

scallop and leek **conchiglie**

Leek adds a subtle flavor to this sophisticated pasta; it pairs with the sweetness of the scallops marvelously, underscoring the elegance of the dish.

serves 4

$1/2$ cup extra-virgin olive oil
$1/4$ cup spicy olive oil
   or 1 dried chili pepper, crumbled
2 garlic cloves, minced
1 leek, white part only, thinly sliced
4 tomatoes, cubed
salt and freshly ground black pepper
1 pound conchiglie
1 pound bay scallops
1 bunch basil, leaves only

In a large sauté pan, heat the olive oil with the spicy olive oil or chili pepper over medium heat. Add the garlic, and cook until golden, about 30 seconds. Fold in the leek and cook until wilted, about 10 minutes over medium heat; stir in the tomatoes, and season with salt and pepper.

   Meanwhile, bring 5 quarts of water to a boil. Add the conchiglie and salt, and cook until al dente; drain, reserving $1/3$ cup of the pasta cooking water.

   Add 2 tablespoons of the reserved pasta cooking water to the leek and tomato sauce in the pan; fold in the scallops, and cover. After 2 minutes, remove the lid and fold in the conchiglie (you may need to add a little more of the reserved pasta cooking water). Sauté for 30 seconds, or until the sauce thickens and coats the conchiglie well; stir in the basil and a little pepper, adjust the salt if needed, and serve hot.

gemelli with smoked trout and pink peppercorns

Gemelli means 'twins' in Italian, and this pasta, in fact, looks like twinned short strands. Gianni marries it with smoked trout, since trout is a favorite fish in Piedmont.

In a large sauté pan, heat the olive oil. Add the chili pepper or spicy olive oil, and warm for 2 minutes. Fold in the onion and cook until it is just wilted, about 5 minutes over medium heat.

Meanwhile, bring 5 quarts of water to a boil. Add the gemelli and salt, and cook until al dente. Drain, reserving $1/3$ cup of the pasta cooking water.

Fold the smoked trout into the onion mixture in the pan, and cook for 1 minute. Raise the heat to medium-high, deglaze the pan with the vodka, and cook until the alcohol has evaporated, about 2 minutes. Stir in the horseradish and Mascarpone, then the gemelli; add some of the reserved pasta cooking water to dilute the sauce until it coats the pasta. Fold in the pink peppercorns, and sauté for 1 minute, allowing the sauce to thicken. Adjust the salt if needed, and serve immediately.

serves 4

$1/4$ cup extra-virgin olive oil

1 dried chili pepper, crumbled, or $1/4$ cup spicy olive oil

1 onion, minced

1 pound gemelli

salt

8 ounces smoked trout, cut diagonally in $1/2$" pieces

$1/2$ cup vodka

4 teaspoons grated fresh horseradish

$1/4$ cup Mascarpone (preferably imported Italian) or heavy cream

1 teaspoon pink peppercorns

eliche with gorgonzola and radicchio

Gorgonzola, a blue-veined cow's milk cheese from Italy, has a slightly pungent quality that is perfect with the bitterness of radicchio. Look for Gorgonzola Dolce (young, creamy Gorgonzola) for best results.

Bring 7 quarts of water to a boil, add the eliche and salt, and cook until al dente. Drain, reserving $1/3$ cup of the pasta cooking water.

Meanwhile, heat the olive oil in a large sauté pan over medium heat. Add the onion and cook until it is just soft and translucent, about 5 minutes. Stir the radicchio into the onion in the pan, and sauté for 1 minute; the radicchio should wilt but still retain its vibrant red color, or the dish will appear dull on the plate.

Toss the eliche into the pan with the radicchio sauce, along with 3 tablespoons of the reserved pasta cooking water, and stir in the Gorgonzola; cook for 1 minute, stirring, until the Gorgonzola melts. The sauce will thicken, so add more of the reserved pasta cooking water as needed to maintain the appropriate consistency. Season with salt and pepper, and dust with the Parmigiano. Serve immediately.

serves 6

20 ounces eliche
salt
$1/4$ cup extra-virgin olive oil
1 small onion, finely chopped
1 head radicchio, cut into strips
4 ounces Gorgonzola Dolce, cubed
freshly ground black pepper
$1/3$ cup freshly grated Parmigiano
    Reggiano

mezze zite with asparagus, fonduta, and truffled olive oil

A classic Piedmontese dish that is ideal for chilly winter nights, and a favorite at Palio d'Asti. To be truly decadent, shave fresh white truffles over the pasta just before serving, suggests Gianni.

Make the fonduta: Place the cubed Fontina in a bowl and pour in the milk; the Fontina should be entirely covered (add more milk if needed). Allow to rest at room temperature for at least 2 to 3 hours.

In a double boiler, melt the butter; add the Fontina and milk, stirring constantly with a wooden spoon until the Fontina is melted. Whisk in the egg yolks and continue to stir vigorously over medium heat, regulating the temperature to avoid curdling. Add more milk if needed to achieve a creamy consistency that will pour easily. Keep hot.

Make the pasta: Bring 7 quarts of water to a boil, add the asparagus and salt, and cook for 2 minutes; remove with a slotted spoon to a bowl of cold water. Return the water to a boil, and add the mezze zite; cook until al dente and drain, reserving 1/3 cup of the pasta cooking water.

Meanwhile, heat the olive oil in a large pan over medium heat. Add the leek, and cook until softened, about 5 minutes. Stir in the asparagus and sauté for 1 minute. Add the mezze zite, pepper, and 3 tablespoons of the reserved pasta cooking water to the asparagus sauce, and cook until the sauce thickens over high heat, adding more of the pasta cooking water if needed.

Remove the pan from the heat, stir in the truffle oil, and spoon the pasta into 6 warm plates. Top each serving with several tablespoons of the fonduta, and serve hot.

serves 6

For the fonduta:
4 ounces Fontina from Val d'Aosta, cubed
2 cups whole milk, plus extra if needed
4 tablespoons unsalted butter
2 egg yolks

For the pasta:
16 pencil-thin asparagus spears, cut on the bias into 1" pieces
salt
20 ounces mezze zite
1/4 cup extra-virgin olive oil
1 small leek, white part only, thinly sliced
freshly ground black pepper
3 tablespoons white truffle oil

Erik Holverson

giuseppe
ferrara

mezze zite with shrimp, spinach,
and curry • crab and lemon tagliolini •
spicy seafood linguine al cartoccio •
swordfish and mint penne •
fettuccine with roasted artichokes
and sun-dried tomatoes

"**Becoming a chef** was not so much a decision as a natural evolution for me," says Giuseppe Ferrara, Executive Chef and proprietor of Amalfi Trattoria in Walnut Creek, California. "I was born in the town of Cava dei Tirreni, near the Amalfi Coast, and excellent food is a way of life there." Giuseppe began his culinary career by cooking meals at the Officers' Club in Rome during a stint in the Italian Air Force. After settling in America in 1979, he worked at San Francisco's O'Sole Mio and Harry's Bar and American Grill. Moving to the East Bay, where the pace was a little slower than in San Francisco proper, he became Executive Chef of Spiedini and Prima Trattoria. Today, he brings the scents and flavors of his native region to California at his just-opened Amalfi Trattoria. The walls of his cozy restaurant are lined with stunning photographs of the Amalfi Coast, which Giuseppe took on a summer visit back home. "Cooking is a creative process. So is photography: with photographs, just like with food, you capture the essence of a place." Giuseppe manages to catch the essence of Amalfi with signature dishes that range from tagliolini with crab and lemon to mezze zite in a curry-scented shrimp and spinach sauce. "I think food is the best way to transport someone to distant shores. And to me, the best shores I can think of are those of the Amalfi Coast."

mezze zite with shrimp, spinach, and curry

Curry powder is sometimes added to Italian dishes like this subtle seafood pasta, but to keep the flavors Italian, remember to use a light touch.

In a sauté pan large enough to accommodate the mezze zite later, heat 1 tablespoon of the olive oil. Add the pine nuts and cook, stirring, for 2 minutes over medium heat; remove to a plate. Heat the remaining olive oil; add the shrimp; cook until pink, turning once, about 2 minutes. Deglaze with the wine, and let it evaporate. Add the broth, cream, butter, curry, salt, and white pepper, and bring to a boil. Cook for 2 minutes over medium-high heat, then remove the shrimp to a plate. Reduce the sauce until creamy, about 5 minutes; you may need to add 1 more tablespoon of butter.

Meanwhile, bring 5 quarts of water to a boil. Add the mezze zite and salt, and cook until al dente. Drain and toss with the sauce in the pan. Fold in the spinach and shrimp; when the spinach wilts, transfer to a platter, sprinkle with the pine nuts, and serve hot.

serves 4

$1/4$ cup extra-virgin olive oil
3 tablespoons pine nuts
20 jumbo shrimp, shelled and deveined
$1/4$ cup dry white wine
$1 1/2$ cups chicken broth (see page 183)
$1/2$ cup heavy cream
1 tablespoon unsalted butter,
    plus extra if needed
1 teaspoon curry powder
salt and freshly ground white pepper
1 pound mezze zite
4 cups baby spinach, washed

crab and lemon **tagliolini**

Giuseppe, a master of fish and seafood cookery thanks to a youth spent on the Amalfi Coast, sometimes substitutes lobster for the crab in this recipe, especially if it happens to be lobster season. The lemon zest is blanched repeatedly in water to mitigate some of its natural bitterness.

Place the lemon zest and 1 cup of water in a small pot, and bring to a boil over medium-high heat. Cook for 2 minutes, then drain, reserving the zest and discarding the water; repeat the boiling procedure 2 more times, replacing the water each time. After the third time, place the lemon zest in a small bowl of cold water. (The repeated blanching process makes the lemon zest less tart and more palatable.) Once cooled, julienne the zest as thinly as possible, and set aside.

In a sauté pan large enough to accommodate the tagliolini later, heat the olive oil and add the garlic; cook until golden, about 30 seconds over medium heat, then fold in the crabmeat. Cook for 2 minutes; deglaze the pan with the wine, and add salt and pepper. Pour in the broth, bring to a boil, and cook for 3 more minutes, or until the liquid in the pan has somewhat reduced.

Meanwhile, bring 5 quarts of water to a boil. Add the tagliolini and salt, and cook until al dente; drain. Fold the tagliolini into the crab sauce along with the reserved lemon zest and the parsley, adjust the salt and pepper if needed, and serve hot.

serves 4

zest of 1 lemon, cut in 2 or 3 large strips
$1/4$ cup extra-virgin olive oil
2 garlic cloves, slivered
1 pound Dungeness crabmeat,
  picked over
$1/4$ cup dry white wine
salt and freshly ground black pepper
1 cup chicken broth (see page 183)
1 pound tagliolini
1 tablespoon minced Italian parsley

spicy seafood **linguine** al cartoccio

Giuseppe bakes linguine with seafood in parchment paper; the result is a tantalizing dish worthy of the most sophisticated dinner. Bring the pasta to the table still enclosed in the parchment paper, and cut the packets in front of your guests: they will be delighted by the aroma emanating from within.

Scrub the mussels and trim off any beards; rinse the clams. Place the mussels and clams in a bowl, cover with water, and add 1 tablespoon of salt; soak for 30 minutes. Drain and rinse. In a large sauté pan, place the mussels and clams; cook over medium heat until the shells open, about 5 minutes (add a little water if needed). Remove the mussels and clams from the shells, and discard the shells.

Bring 5 quarts of water to a boil. Add the squid and salt; cook for 2 minutes, or until the squid is firm to the touch and no longer translucent, being careful not to overcook it or it will turn rubbery. Remove with a slotted spoon to a plate and set aside; keep the water boiling.

Sauté the cherry tomatoes with the olive oil, garlic, and chili in the pan in which you cooked the mussels and clams for 5 minutes, or until the tomatoes start to break down into a sauce. Add the fish, squid, and shrimp, and cook 30 seconds; deglaze with the wine and cook for 5 minutes. Fold in the mussels, clams, parsley, fennel seeds, and salt.

serves 4

1 pound black mussels
1 pound Manila clams
salt
6 ounces cleaned squid, bodies
   cut into rings and tentacles halved
8 ounces cherry tomatoes, halved
$1/4$ cup extra-virgin olive oil
4 garlic cloves, minced
1 teaspoon chili flakes
8 ounces boneless and skinless
   whitefish, sea bass, or red snapper,
   cut into 1" cubes
8 jumbo shrimp, shelled and deveined
$1/2$ cup dry white wine
1 tablespoon minced Italian parsley
1 teaspoon crushed fennel seeds
$1/2$ teaspoon saffron
1 pound linguine
4 sheets parchment paper
   (each cut into a 12" square)
1 egg white, beaten to blend

Meanwhile, preheat the oven to 400°. Add the saffron to the reserved boiling water. Add the linguine; cook until al dente. Drain, then toss with the sauce. Divide the pasta into 4 equal portions, and place each portion in the center of 1 piece of parchment paper. Roll the edges to seal, brushing first with the egg white; place the packets on a baking sheet. Bake 5 minutes. Serve hot, opening the packets at the table.

swordfish and mint

penne
Decidedly Sicilian in inspiration, this dish is best made with fragrant, just-plucked mint from a garden; avoid dried mint, which has a dusty flavor and lacks the brightness necessary for this sauce. Clearly a Ferrara signature dish, another exuberant celebration of fresh Mediterranean fish.

In a skillet, heat the olive oil over medium heat and add the garlic. Cook the garlic until it is just golden around the edges but not dark, about 30 seconds; add the cherry tomatoes, swordfish, caper berries or capers, salt, and pepper. Cook for 5 minutes, stirring often, and then deglaze with the wine. Cook for 5 more minutes over medium-high heat, or until the wine evaporates and the swordfish is done. Using a fork, puncture some of the cherry tomatoes to release their juices into the sauce.

Meanwhile, bring 5 quarts of water to a boil. Add the penne and salt, and cook until al dente; drain and fold into the sauce. Sauté for 1 minute to combine the flavors, stir in the mint, adjust the salt if necessary, and serve hot.

serves 4

$^1/_4$ cup extra-virgin olive oil

4 garlic cloves, slivered

10 ounces cherry tomatoes

12 ounces skinless swordfish,
   cut into 2"-wide strips

2 tablespoons caper berries
   or 1 tablespoon capers

salt and freshly ground black pepper

$^1/_4$ cup dry white wine

1 pound penne

$^1/_2$ cup mint leaves, chopped

fettuccine with roasted artichokes and sun-dried tomatoes

If you have a barbecue in your back yard, use it to grill the artichokes for this delectable dish. Otherwise you can simply opt for a heated cast iron grill pan or a preheated broiler.

Trim the tops, stems, and outer leaves of the baby artichokes, and drop each artichoke into a bowl of cold water combined with the juice of $1/2$ lemon as soon as it is trimmed. When all the artichokes are ready, drain them and place them in a pot with 2 quarts of cold water, the juice of $1/2$ lemon, the thyme, bay leaves, wine, 2 tablespoons of the olive oil, one-third of the garlic, and 1 teaspoon of salt. Bring to a rapid boil and cook until the artichokes are crisp-tender, about 10 minutes. Drain the artichokes and cool on a cookie sheet. Spear 9 artichokes on each of 4 skewers, arrange on a baking sheet, and drizzle with 1 tablespoon of the olive oil. Place the skewers on a hot barbecue or grill, or in a preheated broiler, and cook until lightly charred on all sides, about 5 minutes, turning once.

In a sauté pan, heat the remaining olive oil and add the remaining garlic; cook until golden and aromatic, about 30 seconds over medium heat. Add the artichokes, chili pepper, sun-dried tomatoes, and broth, and bring to a boil; cook until the liquid reduces slightly, about 2 minutes. Remove from the heat and adjust the salt.

Meanwhile, bring 5 quarts of water to a boil. Add the fettuccine and salt, and cook until al dente; drain, and fold into the sauce in the pan along with the arugula. Turn out into a serving platter, fold in the reserved oil from the sun-dried tomatoes, and stir in the remaining lemon juice. Serve hot.

serves 4

36 baby artichokes
juice of $1\frac{1}{2}$ lemons
5 thyme sprigs
2 bay leaves
$1/4$ cup dry white wine
5 tablespoons extra-virgin olive oil
4 garlic cloves, slivered
salt
1 dried chili pepper, crumbled
1 cup julienned, oil-preserved sun-dried tomatoes, oil reserved
1 cup chicken or vegetable broth (see page 183 or 184)
1 pound fettuccine
2 bunches arugula, stems removed, washed

luca **filadi**

garganelli with lamb ragù • bucatini with mussels and herb-infused oil • orange-laced linguine with olives • stuffed mezze maniche in chickpea broth • orecchiette with cabbage and gorgonzola

Some chefs look to expensive ingredients to hook their clientele. Others search out complicated techniques to wow their audience. Not so Luca Filadi, a native of the Veneto who would just as soon cook chickpeas and lentils as scampi and caviar. Trained at the Culinary Institute in Salsomaggiore Terme and at L'École Lenôtre in Paris, Luca discovered his passion and talent for food while working in his family's restaurant near Vicenza. After a stint at London's renowned Harry's Bar, Luca moved to Manhattan, where he is currently Executive Chef at Gubbio Restaurant. His mission: to offer patrons traditional Umbrian dishes of earthy simplicity. "I use the best lentils in the world, those from Castelluccio, to make soups and pasta sauces, and to accompany roasted pork and so on. I feature farro, chickpeas, and hand-cut pastas on my menu. I don't believe an ingredient has to be costly to be delicious," he explains. Luca's favorite pastas reflect his approach to cuisine: tubes are stuffed with bread crumbs and herbs, then dropped into a chickpea broth; garganelli are napped with a rich lamb ragù underscored by star anise. "It's all in the flavoring," he concludes.

garganelli with lamb ragù

An unusual ragù scented with star anise pairs with Emilia-Romagna's famed garganelli. Add a touch of minced parsley at the end for color.

Make the lamb: Combine all the ingredients except the butter, olive oil, and salt in a large bowl. Toss well to distribute the flavors, and marinate in the refrigerator for 24 to 48 hours, turning every few hours to better allow the marinade to penetrate the meat. When you are ready to cook the ragù, divide the ingredients into 3 separate bowls: Place the lamb in one, the vegetables and herbs in another, and the liquid in a third. Cube the meat into ¼" pieces and set aside.

In a large sauté pan, heat the butter and 2 tablespoons of the olive oil. Add the vegetables and herbs, and cook until lightly browned in spots, about 10 minutes over medium heat, stirring often.

In a separate skillet, heat the remaining olive oil. Sear the lamb on all sides, turning often with tongs to cook evenly; it will take about 6 minutes. Tip out any fat remaining in the pan, and add the lamb to the vegetables in the other pan. Deglaze the pan with the reserved liquid from the marinade. Bring to a boil, then lower the heat and simmer for 1½ hours, covered, or until the lamb is tender. Season with salt.

Make the pasta: Bring 5 quarts of water to a boil. Add the garganelli and salt, and cook until the garganelli are al dente. Drain, return to the pot, and fold in the ragù. Discard the bay leaves, thyme sprigs, and star anise, and serve hot.

serves 4

For the lamb:
24 ounces boneless lamb shoulder, cut into 4 pieces
2 celery stalks, minced
2 carrots, minced
8 shallots, minced
1 bunch Italian parsley, leaves only, minced
freshly ground black pepper
2 bay leaves
2 thyme sprigs
1 star anise
⅛ teaspoon freshly grated nutmeg
4 cups dry red wine
4 tablespoons unsalted butter
¾ cup extra-virgin olive oil
salt
For the pasta:
1 pound garganelli
salt

bucatini with mussels and herb-infused oil

Parsley, scallions, fennel, capers, and garlic are minced together and infused in olive oil to provide a flavorful backdrop for the mussels in this gutsy dish.

Make the mussels: Scrub the mussels and remove any beards that are still clinging with a small paring knife. Place in a bowl, cover with cold water, and add 1 tablespoon of salt; soak for 30 minutes, then drain and rinse.

Heat the olive oil in a large pan, add the garlic, thyme, and mussels, and cook over medium heat for 2 minutes. Pour in the wine and cover; cook until the mussels have opened, about 5 minutes, then remove them from their shells and collect their cooking juices. Strain the cooking juices through a filter-lined sieve and set aside.

Make the herb mixture: Mince the parsley, scallions, fennel, capers, and garlic together on a cutting board, or pulse to mince in a food processor; toss with 2 tablespoons of the olive oil in a small bowl.

Heat the remaining olive oil in the pan you used to cook the mussels, and add the mussels and their reserved cooking juices. Fold in the herb mixture, and season with salt and pepper. Keep warm.

Make the pasta: Bring 5 quarts of water to a boil. Add the bucatini and salt; cook until al dente. Drain, and toss into the pan with the sauce. Adjust the seasoning if needed, and serve the bucatini hot.

serves 4

For the mussels:
1 pound mussels
salt
$1/4$ cup extra-virgin olive oil
4 garlic cloves, minced
1 teaspoon minced thyme
$1/2$ cup dry white wine
For the herb mixture:
3 bunches Italian parsley, leaves only, chopped
3 scallions, chopped
$1/2$ fennel bulb, trimmed and chopped
$1/3$ cup capers
$1/2$ garlic clove, peeled
$1/4$ cup extra-virgin olive oil
salt and freshly ground black pepper
For the pasta:
1 pound bucatini
salt

orange-laced **linguine** with olives

In this innovative pasta, Luca pairs two contrasting elements—orange zest and olives—to great effect. The ingredients for the sauce can be found in most refrigerators, so this is an ideal dish for an impromptu dinner with friends.

Bring 5 quarts of water to a boil, add the linguine and salt, and cook until al dente; drain, reserving ⅓ cup of the pasta cooking water.

Meanwhile, heat the olive oil in a sauté pan large enough to accommodate the linguine later. Cook the garlic in the olive oil until it takes on a golden color and nutty aroma, about 30 seconds over medium heat; add the olives and orange zest, and cook for 2 more minutes. Pour in the wine and continue to cook until the wine nearly evaporates, about 3 minutes.

Toss the linguine with the sauce in the pan, adding a little of the reserved pasta cooking water to dilute the sauce if necessary. Adjust the salt as needed, turn out into a heated serving bowl, and garnish with the parsley. Sprinkle with the freshly ground black pepper and serve hot.

serves 4

1 pound linguine
salt
2 tablespoons extra-virgin olive oil
1 garlic clove, chopped
1 cup pitted black olives, chopped
grated zest of 1 orange
½ cup dry white wine
1 tablespoon chopped Italian parsley
freshly ground black pepper

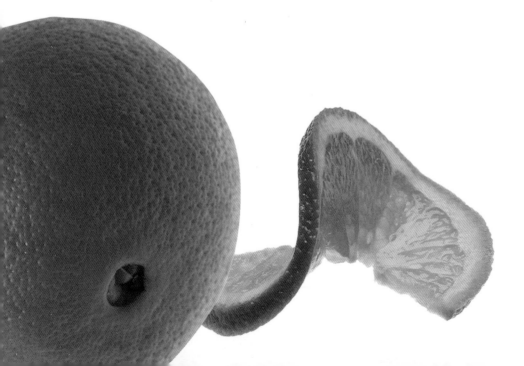

stuffed **mezze maniche** in chickpea broth
Original, soothing, and nutritious, this soupy pasta is best savored after a chilly afternoon raking leaves in the yard.

serves 6

2 leeks, white part only, chopped
8 shallots, chopped
1/4 cup extra-virgin olive oil
6 tablespoons unsalted butter
1 pound dry chickpeas, soaked in water
  to cover for 12 hours and drained
3 cups vegetable broth (see page 184),
  plus extra if needed
2 rosemary sprigs
salt
1 pound mezze maniche
2 cups freshly grated Parmigiano
  Reggiano
1/2 cup fresh bread crumbs
1/4 teaspoon freshly grated nutmeg
1/2 teaspoon minced thyme
freshly ground black pepper
3 eggs

Pound the leeks and shallots in a mortar until a paste forms. Heat 2 tablespoons of the olive oil and all of the butter in a sauté pan, and add the leek and shallot paste; cook until aromatic, about 5 minutes over medium heat.

Add the drained chickpeas, and cook for 10 minutes. Pour in the broth; it should cover the chickpeas (if it does not, add more broth). Add the rosemary, bring to a boil, and simmer for 2 hours. When the chickpeas are tender, discard the rosemary and blend the chickpeas and their cooking liquid until smooth in a blender; the texture should be soupy, not thick (if it is thick, add broth). Season with salt, and set aside.

Meanwhile, bring 5 quarts of water to a boil. Add the mezze maniche and salt, and cook until the pasta is just a little over half cooked. Drain and cool.

To make the stuffing, combine 1 1/2 cups of the Parmigiano, the bread crumbs, nutmeg, thyme, pepper, and eggs in a bowl; using a small spoon, push some of this stuffing into the boiled mezze maniche. Bring the chickpea soup up to a boil. Drop the stuffed mezze maniche into the soup, and cook until the mezze maniche are done, about 3 minutes. Adjust the salt if needed, spoon into 6 heated bowls, drizzle with the remaining olive oil, and sprinkle with the remaining Parmigiano. Serve hot.

orecchiette with cabbage and gorgonzola

Sultry winter fare at its best: a Southern Italian pasta (orecchiette) meets a blue-veined Northern Italian cheese (Gorgonzola) and a Northern Italian vegetable (Savoy cabbage) in this creamy dish.

Heat the olive oil and butter in a sauté pan large enough to accommodate the orecchiette later, and add the scallions; cook until the scallions begin to wilt, about 2 minutes over medium heat. Add the thyme and cabbage, and cook for 20 more minutes, stirring once in a while to prevent sticking; add a touch of water if the mixture dries out too much. Pour in the wine, and cook until it evaporates, about 3 minutes.

Meanwhile, bring 5 quarts of water to a boil. Add the orecchiette and salt, and cook until al dente (check the package instructions: it should take about 15 to 20 minutes). Drain, reserving 1/2 cup of the pasta cooking water, and toss the orecchiette into the pan with the cabbage sauce.

Fold in the Gorgonzola, and season with salt and pepper, taking care not to oversalt the dish since the Gorgonzola is already quite salty. Sauté long enough to lightly melt the Gorgonzola, adding some of the reserved pasta cooking water if needed to thin out the sauce. Transfer to a heated serving platter, garnish with the parsley and Parmigiano, and serve hot.

serves 4

1/3 cup extra-virgin olive oil
6 tablespoons unsalted butter
3 scallions, minced
1 teaspoon minced thyme
1 small head Savoy cabbage,
   cut into 1/2"-wide strips
1/2 cup dry white wine
1 pound orecchiette
salt
12 ounces Gorgonzola Dolce, cubed
freshly ground black pepper
1 tablespoon minced Italian parsley
1/2 cup freshly grated Parmigiano
   Reggiano

John Hale

marcelo
gallegos

rock shrimp spaghetti • fettuccine and figs • lasagne with three-meat ragù • artichoke and mascarpone tagliatelle • mafaldine with veal and tomato

Born to Mexican parents, Chicago-native Marcelo Gallegos has adopted Italy as his home country. "Ever since I watched the table scenes in the 'Godfather' movies, I became fascinated with the key role that food plays in Italian culture. And so I decided to become an Italian chef," explains Gallegos. Executive Chef of Chicago's famed Vivere Restaurant, Marcelo earned his culinary stripes in Italy's top restaurants: "I spent time at the Michelin three-star Ristorante Dal Pescatore, where Nadia Santini taught me so much, especially about fresh pasta." Today, Gallegos offers guests at Vivere an amazing variety of Italian dishes, straying from tradition only to surprise and tease the palate. Among his creations: pheasant ravioli in butter-sage sauce; saffron noodles with seared salmon, cinnamon, and pomegranate; and roasted Guinea hen with foie gras and blackberry marmalade. Marcelo believes that to stay "fresh and interesting," he has to continuously discover culinary trends. "I go to Italy with Alfredo Capitanini, one of the owners of Vivere, at least once a year, just to keep on top of what's happening in Italy. We spend weeks eating, eating, and eating in the best restaurants, then come back and work on the menu. That first-hand taste experience keeps us on the cutting edge."

rock shrimp **spaghetti** Rock shrimp
are sweeter and milder in flavor than other shrimp; they are usually sold already shelled, and are available at most well-stocked fish markets. If you cannot obtain them in your area, use regular shrimp.

Combine the fish and chicken broths with the wine in a large pot and bring to a boil; reduce to about 1 cup. It will take about 20 minutes over medium heat.

Meanwhile, in a sauté pan, heat the olive oil over medium heat; add the garlic and cook until it begins to brown, about 30 seconds, then discard the garlic. Raise the heat to high, and add the onion, parsley, rosemary, and sage; cook just until the onion becomes translucent, about 5 minutes. Turn off the heat and discard the parsley, rosemary, and sage; season with salt and keep warm.

Raise the heat under the onion to medium-high. Stir the shrimp and chili flakes into the onion, and cook for 30 seconds. Add the reduced broth-wine mixture, and cook for another 30 seconds. Stir in the tomatoes, olives, and pepper, and cook over high heat for another 45 seconds; the shrimp should just be tender and pink (do not overcook them or they will turn rubbery).

While the sauce cooks, bring 5 quarts of water to a boil. Add the spaghetti and salt, and cook until al dente. Drain. Stir the spaghetti into the sauce, turn the heat down to medium, and add the lemon juice. Adjust the salt and pepper, and serve hot.

serves 6

1 cup fish broth (see page 184)
2 1/2 cups chicken broth (see page 183)
3/4 cup dry white wine
1/3 cup extra-virgin olive oil
2 garlic cloves, minced
1/2 onion, finely chopped
8 Italian parsley sprigs
2 rosemary sprigs
3 sage leaves
salt
12 ounces rock shrimp,
    shelled and deveined
1/8 teaspoon chili flakes
2 cups canned strained plum tomatoes
1 cup pitted black olives, chopped
freshly ground black pepper
1 pound spaghetti
juice of 1/2 lemon

fettuccine and figs
A very original dish that takes advantage of the sweetness and gorgeous good looks of fresh figs. Marcelo uses a bit of grated lemon zest to lend a tart, citrusy note to the cream sauce, and the result is pure magic.

In a sauté pan large enough to accommodate the fettuccine later, melt the butter. Add the grated lemon zest and cook until fragrant, about 45 seconds over medium heat. Add the figs and the chili flakes, stir, and raise the heat to medium-high; cook for 1 minute, or until the figs are lightly browned in spots, being careful not to bruise the figs as they cook.

Lower the heat to medium once again, and pour in the cream. Bring to a boil and cook for 2 minutes, or until reduced; the sauce should coat the back of a spoon.

Meanwhile, bring 5 quarts of water to a boil. Add the fettuccine and salt, and cook until al dente; drain. Toss the fettuccine with the fig sauce in the pan, fold in the Parmigiano, season with salt and pepper, and serve immediately.

serves 6

1 stick (8 tablespoons) unsalted butter
grated zest of $1/4$ lemon
13 large fresh figs, chopped (peel on)
$1/8$ teaspoon chili flakes
1 cup plus 2 tablespoons heavy cream
1 pound fettuccine
salt
1 cup plus 2 tablespoons freshly grated
   Parmigiano Reggiano
freshly ground black pepper

lasagne with three-meat

ragù Marcelo contrasts gamy venison, boar, and rabbit with sweet spices like nutmeg and cinnamon and fragrant herbs like rosemary, thyme, and sage.

serves 6

$1/4$ cup extra-virgin olive oil
1 onion, finely chopped
1 carrot, finely chopped
12 ounces boneless wild boar,
   trimmed and cut into $1/2$" cubes
12 ounces boneless venison,
   trimmed and cut into $1/2$" cubes
12 ounces boneless rabbit,
   trimmed and cut into $1/2$" cubes
salt and freshly ground black pepper
1 garlic clove, minced
1 teaspoon minced rosemary
1 teaspoon minced thyme
1 teaspoon minced sage
1 tablespoon tomato paste
$1/8$ teaspoon freshly grated nutmeg
$1/8$ teaspoon ground cinnamon
$1/4$ cup red wine vinegar
$3/4$ cup dry white wine
3 cups beef broth (see page 183),
   plus extra if needed
1 pound lasagne
$1/2$ cup freshly grated Parmigiano
   Reggiano

In a sauté pan large enough to accommodate all the meat in a single layer, heat the olive oil over medium-high heat. Add the onion and carrot, and cook for 5 minutes, or until onion is golden but not browned and the carrot has begun to soften. Add the boar, venison, and rabbit to the pan, keeping them in a single layer to encourage browning. Sprinkle with the salt and pepper, and cook for 30 minutes, or until evenly browned all over, stirring often. Stir in the garlic, rosemary, thyme, and sage, and cook for 2 minutes. Add the tomato paste, nutmeg, cinnamon, and vinegar; cook for 1 minute, or until the vinegar loses its pungent, sharp smell. Pour in the wine, and cook until the alcohol has evaporated, about 3 minutes. Add the broth, and lower the heat; simmer for $1^3/4$ to $2^1/2$ hours, adding broth as needed to keep the meat from drying out and stirring every 30 minutes or so.

   Meanwhile, bring 5 quarts water to a boil. Add the lasagne and salt, and cook until al dente. Drain; return to the pot, toss well with the ragù, and spoon into 6 heated bowls. Serve hot, sprinkled with the Parmigiano.

artichoke and mascarpone
tagliatelle
A decadent dollop of Mascarpone—a fresh, creamy, spreadable cheese—sits atop this lovely vegetable pasta.

Trim the artichokes by removing the tough outer leaves, cutting off the stems and top third, and scooping out the hairy inner choke; slice into paper-thin slices. Immediately drop into a bowl of water acidulated with the lemon juice. This prevents the artichokes from turning black.

Heat a sauté pan large enough to accommodate the tagliatelle later over medium-high heat. Add the butter and olive oil, then drop in the drained artichokes, stirring to coat them with the butter and oil. Cook until tender, about 10 minutes, lowering the heat if necessary so they do not become dark. Deglaze with the broth, bring to a boil, and cook over medium heat until the liquid reduces by half, about 5 minutes.

Meanwhile, bring 5 quarts of water to a boil. Add the tagliatelle and salt, and cook until al dente; drain and toss in the pan with the artichokes. Cook for 1 minute, allowing the sauce to thicken, and season with salt and pepper. Spoon into 6 bowls.

Top each portion with some of the Mascarpone, the basil, and the Parmigiano, and serve immediately.

serves 6

6 large artichokes
juice of 1$\frac{1}{2}$ lemons
2 tablespoons unsalted butter
1 teaspoon extra-virgin olive oil
$\frac{1}{2}$ cup chicken broth (see page 183)
1 pound tagliatelle
salt and freshly ground black pepper
8 ounces Mascarpone
    (preferably imported Italian)
16 basil leaves, torn
$\frac{1}{4}$ cup freshly grated Parmigiano
    Reggiano

mafaldine with veal and tomato
Marcelo uses a combination of fresh tomatoes and canned tomatoes for this sauce to achieve the right consistency and level of acidity.

Heat the olive oil in a sauté pan over medium heat. Add the carrot, celery, and onion, and cook for 10 minutes, or until the onion is light in color and soft. Stir in the veal, lower the heat to medium-low, and cook for 20 to 25 minutes, or until the veal is golden brown, stirring often.

Season with the salt, pepper, and thyme, and cook for 5 more minutes over medium heat. Deglaze with the wine, and as it evaporates, scrape the bottom of the pan with a wooden spoon. Fold in half of the plum tomatoes and break them down by stirring with the spoon.

Pour in the broth, and bring the mixture to a boil; lower the heat and simmer for 1³/₄ to 2¹/₄ hours, or until the veal is tender and the sauce is reduced. As the sauce cooks, you may need to add a little more chicken broth to keep the sauce moist.

Stir in the remaining plum tomatoes and all of the canned tomatoes, and cook for another 5 to 10 minutes.

Meanwhile, bring 5 quarts of water to a boil, and cook the mafaldine with salt until al dente; drain. Return the mafaldine to the pot, fold in the ragù, and adjust the salt if necessary. Serve hot, sprinkled with the Parmigiano.

serves 6

1/4 cup extra-virgin olive oil
1 carrot, finely chopped
1 celery stalk, finely chopped
1 onion, finely chopped
1 pound ground veal shoulder
salt and freshly ground black pepper
1 tablespoon chopped thyme
1/2 cup dry white wine
5 plum tomatoes, peeled
   and cut into eighths
1 cup chicken broth (see page 183),
   plus extra if needed
1 1/2 cups canned strained plum tomatoes
1 pound mafaldine
1 cup freshly grated Parmigiano Reggiano

whole wheat spaghetti with mushrooms and pesto • penne with radicchio, pancetta, and balsamic vinegar • mamma francesca's artichoke and shrimp elicoidali • rigatoni alla garfagnana • shrimp and almond spaghetti

rossano
giannini

North Americans have long had a love affair with Tuscany. Lucky for Rossano Giannini, a native of the Tuscan town of Lucca who has been preparing his region's delicacies since graduating from culinary school at Montecatini Terme. Giannini's taste for travel took him as far away as Egypt, where he cooked for diplomats and an upscale business clientele and further perfected his culinary techniques. As his reputation grew, Giannini decided to move to New York. After serving as Executive Chef of Manhattan's Torre di Pisa, Giannini and his wife Maureen ventured out and opened their own restaurant, Lanterna Tuscan Bistro, in the sleepy town on Nyack, on the shores of the Hudson River, in April 2000. When he isn't busy running the American chapter of the Federation of Italian Chefs of America and promoting Italian cuisine throughout the United States, Rossano spends his time overseeing the kitchen staff at Lanterna and researching Tuscan dishes for his ever-changing menu. "Tuscany is my home, and that's where my heart lies. I want to share its flavors with Americans, to offer distinct regional dishes that will thrill and surprise my guests." His most requested dishes at Lanterna are pasta in a heady artichoke, shrimp, and caper sauce; spaghetti topped with shrimp and slivered almonds; and ricotta-and-spinach-stuffed Florentine crêpes in tomato sauce, all of which he proudly teaches students to make in interactive, hands-on cooking classes.

whole wheat **spaghetti** with mushrooms and pesto

For truly delicious pesto, always stir the grated cheese in by hand, and never subject the pesto to heat or the basil will turn dark and bitter.

serves 6

$2^{1}/_{4}$ cups extra-virgin olive oil
5 garlic cloves, 2 minced and 3 peeled
$^{1}/_{2}$ onion, minced
3 pounds shiitake mushrooms, sliced
1 tablespoon minced rosemary
2 teaspoons minced thyme
2 cups dry white wine
3 cups vegetable broth (see page 184)
1 bunch basil, leaves only
$^{1}/_{4}$ cup pine nuts
$^{1}/_{3}$ cup freshly grated Parmigiano Reggiano
1 pound whole wheat spaghetti

Prepare the sauce: In a saucepan, heat $^{1}/_{4}$ cup of the olive oil. Add the minced garlic and onion, and sauté until golden, about 5 minutes over medium heat. Stir in the mushrooms and cook for 5 more minutes, or until the mushrooms begin to soften. Add the rosemary and thyme, and stir to combine. Deglaze with the wine, bring to a boil, and add the vegetable broth. Lower the heat to a simmer and cook for 15 more minutes, or until the liquid has reduced. Keep warm.

Meanwhile, prepare the pesto: In a blender, combine the basil, pine nuts, and peeled garlic cloves until they form a paste. With the blender running, add the remaining olive oil in a steady drizzle until it is incorporated; the pesto should emulsify. Remove from the blender, turn out into a bowl, and stir in the Parmigiano with a fork.

Bring 5 quarts of water to a boil. Add the spaghetti and salt, and cook until al dente; drain. Toss the spaghetti with the mushroom sauce in the pan, remove from the heat, and gently incorporate the pesto. Serve immediately.

penne with radicchio, pancetta, and balsamic vinegar

Look for aged balsamic vinegar (at least ten years old) for this dish; the older the balsamic vinegar, the sweeter and more complex it becomes.

Bring 5 quarts of water to a boil. Add the penne and salt, and cook until the penne are nearly, but not quite, al dente (they will finish cooking in the sauce); drain.

Meanwhile, heat the olive oil in a saucepan large enough to accommodate the penne later. Add the garlic, onion, and pancetta, and cook for 5 minutes over medium heat; the pancetta should just turn golden and the fat should melt.

Add the penne to the sauce in the pan and cook for 1 minute. Fold in the radicchio, and sauté for 3 more minutes; the radicchio should wilt but still retain its bright color. Pour in the balsamic vinegar, sauté 1 minute longer, to mingle the flavors and allow the sauce to grab onto the penne, and serve hot.

serves 4

1 pound penne
salt
2 tablespoons extra-virgin olive oil
1 garlic clove, minced
$^1/_4$ white onion, chopped
4 ounces pancetta, diced
2 heads radicchio, chopped
$^1/_4$ cup balsamic vinegar

mamma francesca's artichoke and shrimp **elicoidali** You can substitute

rigatoni or fusilli rigati for the elicoidali if the latter are difficult to find, but do use a stout, ridged pasta to grab onto the sauce.

Trim the artichokes and cut them into wedges; immediately drop into a bowl of cold water acidulated with the lemon juice.

In a pan large enough to accommodate the elicoidali later, heat the olive oil. Add the garlic and cook until golden, about 30 seconds over medium-high heat. Stir in the shrimp and drained artichoke wedges, and cook for 3 minutes, or until the shrimp turn pink. Deglaze with the wine and cook until it evaporates, about 2 minutes. Add the tomatoes, capers, salt, and pepper, and cook 2 more minutes.

Meanwhile, bring 5 quarts of water to a boil. Add the elicoidali and salt, and cook until al dente; drain. Toss the elicoidali in the pan with the sauce, and adjust the salt and pepper if necessary. Stir in the basil, and serve immediately.

serves 6

8 artichokes
juice of 1 lemon
$1/4$ cup extra-virgin olive oil
2 garlic cloves, minced
30 medium shrimp, shelled and deveined
$1/4$ cup dry white wine
4 plum tomatoes, chopped
2 tablespoons capers
salt and freshly ground black pepper
1 pound elicoidali
1 cup basil leaves, torn

rigatoni alla garfagnana The name of

this recipe refers to a mountainous area of Western Tuscany, where some of the best farro (emmer wheat) is grown and where the local cuisine reflects a love of the land. It is a country dish, with bold, gutsy flavors that Rossano is especially fond of. The rosemary sprig that lends its subtle perfume is a favorite Tuscan touch.

Soak the porcini mushrooms in a bowl of cold water to cover for at least 1 hour; drain, rinse, and set aside (reserve the soaking water for soups or risottos, straining it through a filter-lined sieve before using it).

Heat 2 tablespoons of the olive oil in a sauté pan; add the veal kidneys and cook for 5 minutes. Tip out the oil and cooking juices, and add the remaining olive oil, garlic, and onion; cook just until the garlic and onion turn a light golden brown, about 5 minutes. Stir in the porcini mushrooms and wine, and cook over medium heat until the liquid has reduced, about 5 minutes. Add the tomatoes, rosemary, salt, and pepper; cook 5 more minutes. Discard the rosemary.

Meanwhile, bring 5 quarts of water to a boil, add the rigatoni and salt, and cook until al dente; drain. Toss the rigatoni with the sauce in the pan, and serve hot.

serves 4

$1/2$ cup dried porcini mushrooms
$1/4$ cup extra-virgin olive oil
2 veal kidneys, diced
2 garlic cloves, chopped
$1/4$ red onion, chopped
$1/4$ cup dry white wine
2 plum tomatoes, diced
1 rosemary sprig
salt and freshly ground black pepper
1 pound rigatoni

shrimp and almond
spaghetti To toast the almonds for this dish, Rossano suggests
you spread the almonds out on a baking sheet and place the baking sheet in a
preheated 350° oven for 5 minutes, or until the almonds take on a golden hue.

Bring 7 quarts of water to a boil, add the spaghetti and salt, and cook until al dente; drain, reserving 1 cup of the pasta cooking water.

Heat the olive oil in a sauté pan large enough to accommodate the spaghetti later, add the garlic, and cook until it becomes a light golden brown, about 45 seconds over medium heat. Stir in the shrimp, and sauté for 2 minutes, or until the shrimp just turn pink. Deglaze with the wine, and add the reserved pasta cooking water; cook 2 minutes longer, or until the liquid reduces by half.

Fold in the spaghetti, remove from the heat, and transfer to a serving dish. Garnish with the parsley and almonds, and serve hot.

serves 6

24 ounces spaghetti
salt
$1/4$ cup extra-virgin olive oil
2 garlic cloves, chopped
30 jumbo shrimp, shelled and deveined
$1/2$ cup dry white wine
$1/4$ cup chopped Italian parsley
$1/4$ cup sliced almonds, toasted

Henry Mc Gill

paul loduca

fettuccine with fried zucchini and
garlic bread crumbs • bucatini
with herbed ricotta • garganelli with
seafood and spinach • zitoni with
wild mushrooms and truffled olive
oil • spicy spaghetti with crispy
pancetta and caramelized onions

"I named my restaurant Vinci because there is no one who comes close to what Leonardo achieved in the Renaissance," says Paul Loduca, Chef and owner of two of Chicago's top Italian restaurants, Vinci and Trattoria Parma. After realizing that he loved cooking—he had grown up working in his father's restaurant—Paul attended Johnson & Wales College, where he obtained a degree in culinary arts, then went on to study restaurant and hotel management at Purdue University. While his schooling taught him what little he didn't already know about working in a kitchen and running a restaurant, it was Paul's natural curiosity that gave him an edge over other struggling young chefs aspiring to open their own restaurants. Today, as a natural outgrowth of his curiosity, Paul regularly hosts historical dinners reviving medieval and Renaissance Italian cuisine at Vinci, and spends what little free time he has reading historical books and recreating ancient dishes. "To really understand a cuisine as rich as Italian cuisine, you have to look back at what people ate over the centuries. Then you can develop an appreciation for the depth of Italian cooking," he says. At Vinci, Paul focuses on refined regional Italian preparations, such as pasta in a robust, chunky wild mushroom sauce. At his more casual Trattoria Parma, the emphasis is on rustic dishes: bucatini are presented with asparagus, black olives, and herbed ricotta, and linguine are tossed with fried zucchini coins and bread crumbs.

fettuccine with fried zucchini and garlic bread crumbs

Despite the seemingly large amount of olive oil in the recipe, most of it is drained off, so the dish is not heavy after all.

serves 4

13 garlic cloves, 12 peeled and 1 minced
1 cup extra-virgin olive oil
3 zucchini, cut into $1/2$"-thick coins
salt and freshly ground black pepper
2 cups chicken broth (see page 183)
$1/4$ teaspoon chili flakes
3 slices country bread, cut into $1/4$" cubes
1 pound fettuccine

Preheat the oven to 350°. In a large sauté pan, cook the peeled garlic cloves in $3/4$ cup of the olive oil over low heat until golden brown all over and slightly softened, about 5 minutes; do not burn the garlic or it will take on an acrid flavor. Remove the garlic cloves from the pan and set aside.

In the same olive oil, cook the zucchini coins until lightly golden all over, about 5 minutes over medium heat. Season with salt and pepper, then remove from the pan; discard any extra oil from the pan as well.

Reheat the pan over medium heat, pour in the broth, and add the chili flakes to the broth; bring the broth to a boil, and cook until it reduces by half. Combine the reduced broth, zucchini, and fried garlic cloves in the pan, and keep this sauce warm.

Toss the bread cubes with the minced garlic and 2 tablespoons of the remaining olive oil, and spread on a baking sheet. Bake until crisp and golden, about 10 minutes, then chop into very small pieces, or process in a food processor until very fine.

Meanwhile, bring 5 quarts of water to a boil. Add the fettuccine and salt, and cook until al dente. Drain and toss with the sauce. Drizzle with the remaining olive oil, and top with the garlic bread crumbs. Serve immediately.

bucatini with herbed ricotta

Paul suggests you buy firm, fresh ricotta at a cheese shop or specialty market, rather than buying the sort sold in plastic containers at supermarkets, which contains too much moisture and has little flavor.

Purée the olives with the capers and $1/4$ cup of the olive oil in a food processor until the mixture is smooth, then remove to a bowl.

Rinse the food processor, then blend the ricotta with the Parmigiano and cream until smooth and creamy; season with the pepper.

Heat the remaining olive oil until warm in a pan large enough to accommodate the bucatini later; add the garlic and cook over medium heat until golden, about 30 seconds. Add the asparagus to the pan, and season with salt and pepper. Sauté for 1 minute, or until the asparagus takes on a glazed, shiny look from the oil; fold in the tomatoes and sauté for 2 more minutes. Adjust the salt and pepper.

In the meantime, bring 5 quarts of water to a boil. Add the bucatini and salt, and cook until al dente; drain, reserving $1/2$ cup of the pasta cooking water.

Fold the basil into the sauce in the pan; when the basil wilts, after about 30 seconds, stir in the bucatini and the olive purée. If the sauce is too dry, stir in some of the reserved pasta cooking water.

Toss for 30 seconds, taste for salt and adjust if needed, and place in a warm serving bowl; top with the ricotta mixture, and serve immediately.

serves 4

12 oil-cured black olives, pitted
1 teaspoon capers
$3/4$ cup extra-virgin olive oil
4 ounces fresh ricotta
$1/4$ cup freshly grated Parmigiano
   Reggiano
2 tablespoons heavy cream
freshly ground black pepper
2 garlic cloves, crushed
1 pound pencil-thin asparagus spears,
   trimmed and cut into $1/2$" pieces on
   the bias
salt
3 plum tomatoes, seeded and diced
1 pound bucatini
10 basil leaves

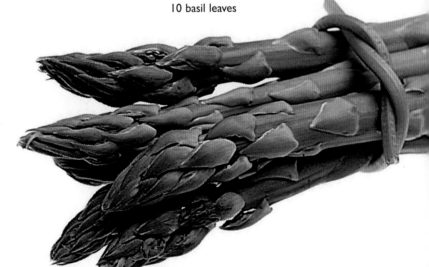

garganelli with seafood and spinach

Emerald green spinach leaves combine with sautéed squid and shrimp in this light seafood pasta. Paul prefers fresh diced plum tomatoes to canned plum tomatoes, especially in the summer, when tomatoes are at their peak.

Cut the eight squid bodies into ¼"-wide strips and halve the tentacles. Heat 3 tablespoons of the olive oil in a large skillet, and sauté the squid bodies and tentacles with the shrimp until the squid and shrimp are opaque, about 3 minutes over medium heat; season with the salt and pepper.

Deglaze with the wine and clam juice or broth, and cook until the liquid in the pan is reduced by two-thirds, about 3 minutes.

In another skillet that is large enough to hold the garganelli, cook the shallot and garlic until the shallot is translucent in the remaining olive oil. Add the tomatoes and spinach to the shallot and garlic in the pan, and cook for about 1 minute, or until the spinach is soft.

In the meantime, bring 5 quarts of water to a boil, and cook the garganelli with salt until al dente. Drain. Fold the garganelli, squid, shrimp, basil, and chives into the tomato sauce in the pan; adjust the salt if needed and serve immediately.

serves 4

8 cleaned squid
⅓ cup extra-virgin olive oil
16 medium shrimp, shelled and deveined
salt and freshly ground black pepper
⅓ cup dry white wine
¼ cup clam juice or fish broth
  (see page 184)
1 shallot, diced
1 garlic clove, minced
2 plum tomatoes, seeded and diced
1 cup spinach leaves,
  washed and roughly chopped
1 pound garganelli
6 basil leaves, torn
1 teaspoon snipped chives

zitoni with wild mushrooms and truffled olive oil
A handful of sliced fresh porcini is a welcome addition to this earthy pasta dish, says Paul. Look for fresh porcini in spring and summer.

serves 4

1 cup dry porcini mushrooms
$^1/_4$ cup extra-virgin olive oil
1 garlic clove, minced
1 teaspoon chopped rosemary
1 teaspoon chopped sage
salt and freshly ground black pepper
1 cup heavy cream
4 tablespoons unsalted butter, cubed
$^1/_4$ cup freshly grated Parmigiano
   Reggiano
1 pound zitoni
1 ounce white truffle oil

Soak the porcini in 2 cups of warm water for 30 minutes; drain, reserving the soaking water and passing it through a filter-lined sieve into a measuring cup or bowl.

In a sauté pan large enough to accommodate the zitoni later, heat the olive oil over medium heat. Add the garlic, rosemary, and sage, and cook for 10 seconds. Add the drained porcini, and season with salt and pepper. When the porcini are tender, after about 5 minutes, pour in the reserved porcini soaking water, and bring to a boil; allow the liquid in the pan to reduce by half, about 5 minutes over medium-high heat. Pour in the cream, and reduce by half once again, about 3 minutes. Whisk in the butter and Parmigiano, and reduce the heat to medium; cook until the sauce is creamy and the Parmigiano has melted, about 1 minute.

Meanwhile, bring 5 quarts of water to a boil. Add the zitoni and salt, and cook until al dente. Drain. Toss the zitoni with the porcini sauce in the pan, using tongs to help you lift the pasta and coat it with the sauce, then drizzle with the truffle oil. Adjust the salt and pepper if necessary, and serve immediately.

spicy **spaghetti** with crispy pancetta and caramelized onions

Paul plays with texture in this creative pasta: he contrasts a mass of soft, wilted onions with crispy pancetta, making each bite a taste explosion.

Heat 2 tablespoons of the olive oil in a 10" skillet over medium-low heat. Add the pancetta and cook until crispy but not dark, about 10 minutes, stirring often. Remove from the pan with a slotted spoon and discard the fat in the skillet.

Heat the remaining olive oil in the same skillet, add the onions and garlic, and cook over medium heat until the onions are caramelized and lightly browned, about 15 minutes, stirring often; remove with a slotted spoon to a plate and set aside.

Add the butter to the skillet, sprinkle in the crushed red pepper, and add the basil; cook until the basil is wilted, about 2 minutes. Pour in the broth, add the Parmigiano and reserved onions and garlic, and cook for 2 minutes.

Meanwhile, bring 5 quarts of water to a boil. Add the spaghetti and salt, and cook until al dente; drain, and toss into the sauce in the skillet. Adjust the seasoning if needed, then transfer to a heated serving bowl. Garnish the top with the crispy pancetta and freshly ground black pepper, and serve hot.

serves 4

$1/4$ cup extra-virgin olive oil
1 pound pancetta, sliced $1/4$" thick and diced
1 pound onions, thinly sliced
1 garlic clove, thinly sliced
4 tablespoons unsalted butter
1 teaspoon crushed red pepper
1 bunch basil, leaves only
$1/4$ cup chicken broth (see page 183)
$1/4$ cup freshly grated Parmigiano Reggiano
1 pound spaghetti
salt and freshly ground black pepper

cold lobster linguine with tarragon-infused olive oil • acorn squash stuffed with mezze penne and shrimp • gramignone with spinach, pancetta, and marjoram • garganelli in many-herb pesto • fusilli with broccolini

maurizio **marfoglia**

"**I was brainwashed** to become a dentist. My father was a dentist, and so it seemed predestined for me too. But to earn some money while I was a student, I lifeguarded in a resort near Venice during the summers, and I started working in a restaurant for fun. I liked it, and so I decided to become a chef," says Maurizio Marfoglia, Executive Chef of Manhattan's posh new innovative Italian restaurant, Revel. A native of Milan and veteran of America's top restaurants—Tribeca Grill, Mad 61, Le Madri, Tuscan Square, and Sette MoMA—thirty-two-year-old Marfoglia has never regretted his decision to leave dentistry and focus on food instead. At Revel, Maurizio has created a stunning array of dishes drawing on Italian techniques and ingredients, all the while incorporating visually striking presentations and novel food pairings. "Food is meant to be fun. I like to get in the kitchen and play, see what I can come up with," he adds. One of his signature items at Revel is chilled linguine with lobster medallions in a subtle, tarragon-infused olive oil; another is crab cakes with orange lentil salad; a third is baby acorn squash stuffed with truffled fonduta. And because half of the fun is in the presentation, Maurizio's tiramisu is brought to the table looking more like an architectural design than a trendy dessert: homemade savoiardi are stacked in a tic-tac-toe pattern on an oversized plate along with a bowl of chilled espresso and a decadent Mascarpone cream for dipping. Who said a classic can't be improved upon?

cold lobster **linguine** with tarragon-infused olive oil

The perfect dish for an elegant buffet: toss everything 1 hour before serving, and let the flavors mingle until it's time for dinner.

Bring 12 quarts of water to a boil in a very large pot. Drop in the lobsters and cook for 12 minutes; drain. When the lobsters are cool enough to handle, crack them open and scoop out the flesh.

Bring 5 quarts of water to a boil in another pot. Drop in the linguine and salt, and cook until al dente; drain. Spread out on a baking sheet and sprinkle with 1 tablespoon of the olive oil.

Place all but 2 sprigs of the tarragon in a blender, removing the stems first, and add the remaining olive oil while the motor is running; the mixture will emulsify and become smooth.

Halve the tomatoes and combine them in a bowl with the salt, pepper, and lemon zest, and allow them to rest for at least 1 hour at room temperature.

Fold the tomatoes into the cold linguine. Add the lobster and toss together like a salad. Pour the tarragon-infused olive oil over the linguine, lobster, and tomatoes, and adjust the seasoning if needed. Divide among 6 pasta bowls, and garnish with the remaining tarragon. Serve within 1 hour.

serves 6

three 1-pound lobsters
1 pound linguine
salt
1 cup extra-virgin olive oil
2 bunches tarragon
12 ounces cherry tomatoes
freshly ground black pepper
grated zest of 1 lemon

acorn squash stuffed with
mezze penne and shrimp

For even greater effect, tuck some of the shrimp around the rim of the squash so they peek out when you bring the dish to the table.

serves 4

5 small acorn squash
salt and freshly ground black pepper
1 small onion, minced
2 garlic cloves, minced
$^1/_3$ cup extra-virgin olive oil
1 pound medium shrimp,
    shelled and deveined
1 teaspoon minced thyme
$^1/_2$ cup dry white wine
1 pound mezze penne
1 tablespoon minced Italian parsley

Preheat the oven to 350°. Cut the tops off each squash and scoop out the seeds from their insides. Sprinkle the inside of 4 of the squash with the salt and pepper, and place the 4 squash upside down on a baking sheet with $^1/_3$ cup of water; bake for 15 minutes. Peel and cube the remaining squash and set aside. Cook the onion and half of the garlic with 2 tablespoons of the olive oil for 5 minutes over medium heat, or until the onion wilts. Fold in the cubed squash and $^1/_4$ cup of water, and cook until the squash is tender, about 10 minutes, stirring often. Remove from the heat, transfer to a blender, purée, and set aside.

In a sauté pan large enough to hold the mezze penne later, cook the remaining garlic clove in 2 tablespoons of the olive oil for 30 seconds over medium heat. Add the shrimp and thyme; cook for 30 seconds; deglaze with the wine and let it evaporate.

Meanwhile, bring 5 quarts of water to a boil; cook the mezze penne with salt until al dente. Drain, and toss with the shrimp and the squash purée in the pan. Adjust the salt, and spoon into the 4 squash. Bake for 20 minutes, then serve hot, sprinkled with the parsley and drizzled with the remaining olive oil.

gramignone with spinach, pancetta, and marjoram

Marjoram is a very powerful herb, so use it sparingly in this sauce: just like sage, cardamom, and saffron, a little goes a long way.

Bring 5 quarts of water to a boil. Add the potato, and cook until it can be pierced with a knife, about 15 minutes; remove with a slotted spoon and peel. Cube and set aside; keep the water boiling. In a large pan, heat all but 1 tablespoon of the olive oil. Add the shallot and garlic, and cook until golden, 2 minutes over medium heat. Stir in the potato, one-third of the spinach, and the marjoram, and cook for 10 more minutes, adding 1 cup of water after 2 minutes. Season with salt. Fold in half of the remaining spinach, and remove to a food processor. Cool; purée until smooth.

In a sauté pan large enough to hold the gramignone later, heat the remaining olive oil. Add the pancetta and cook until crispy, 3 minutes over medium heat. Discard the oil, add the chickpeas and the puréed spinach, and cook for 2 minutes. Fold in the remaining raw spinach; stir until wilted.

Meanwhile, cook the gramignone until al dente in the reserved boiling water. Drain and toss with the sauce. Fold in the Parmigiano, and transfer to a bowl. Serve hot.

serves 4

1 small potato
1/2 cup extra-virgin olive oil
1 shallot, minced
1 garlic clove, minced
1 pound spinach, stems on,
    washed thoroughly
1 marjoram sprig, minced
salt
2 ounces pancetta, cut into strips
1 cup cooked chickpeas (canned are fine)
1 pound gramignone
1/2 cup freshly grated Parmigiano
    Reggiano

garganelli in many-herb
pesto Trofie are a lovely alternative to the garganelli.
Maurizio sometimes adds scampi tails to this dish to make it more opulent.

Bring 5 quarts of water to a boil, add the garganelli and salt, and cook until the garganelli are al dente. Drain.

Meanwhile, combine the basil, mint, oregano, tarragon, dill, garlic, pine nuts, and sugar in a blender; with the motor running, beat in $1/2$ cup of the olive oil in a steady drizzle, and process until emulsified. Make sure not to blend the mixture for too long, otherwise you will inadvertently warm the herbs and oil, killing the fresh flavor of the herbs and turning them black.

Transfer the mixture to a large serving bowl, fold in the Parmigiano and Pecorino, and incorporate the remaining olive oil. Toss the garganelli with the herb pesto, adjust the salt if necessary, and serve immediately.

serves 4

1 pound garganelli
salt
1 bunch basil, leaves only
2 mint sprigs, leaves only
2 oregano sprigs, leaves only
2 tarragon sprigs, leaves only
1 dill sprig, leaves only
2 garlic cloves, peeled
$1/4$ cup pine nuts
1 teaspoon sugar
$3/4$ cup extra-virgin olive oil
$1/4$ cup freshly grated Parmigiano
   Reggiano
$1/4$ cup freshly grated Pecorino Romano

fusilli with broccolini

Maurizio features broccolini, a hybrid created by crossing broccoli with Chinese kale by vegetable growers in California, in this easy-to-put-together pasta.

In a pan large enough to hold the fusilli later, heat 2 tablespoons of the olive oil with half of the garlic and all of the parsley; cook until the garlic is golden brown, about 30 seconds, and then add the broccolini and salt. Cook for 2 minutes, stirring often, then deglaze with the wine. Cover; simmer for 15 minutes, or until wine evaporates and the broccolini is soft.

Combine the remaining garlic with the bread crumbs, lemon zest, and Pecorino in a bowl; add the remaining olive oil, and set aside.

Meanwhile, bring 5 quarts of water to a boil. Add the fusilli and salt, and cook until al dente, then drain. Toss with the broccolini in the pan, fold in the lemon juice and pepper, and transfer the fusilli to a serving bowl. Sprinkle the fusilli with the bread crumb mixture, and serve immediately.

serves 4

$1/3$ cup extra-virgin olive oil
2 garlic cloves, minced
1 bunch Italian parsley, leaves only, chopped
1 pound broccolini, chopped
salt
1 cup dry white wine
1 cup fresh bread crumbs
grated zest of 1 lemon
$1/2$ cup freshly grated Pecorino Romano
1 pound fusilli
juice of $1/2$ lemon
freshly ground black pepper

bruce mcmillian

linguine, crab, and lobster mushrooms in spumante reduction • chilled capellini, scampi, and asparagus in a zesty lemon essence • fettuccelle and baby octopus in lemon-basil pesto • orecchiette with rabbit, broccoli raab, shaved garlic, and porcini • rigatoni with roasted red and yellow peppers, sausage, and barolo

What Bruce McMillian calls "a natural flair" for cooking, most people would call genius. For the last eighteen years, Bruce has studied with and cooked for Tony Vallone, one of Texas' most influential restaurateurs, working his way up in the ranks since the young age of nineteen. He eventually took over the kitchen of each restaurant in the Vallone Restaurant Group, and is currently Executive Chef at Tony's Restaurant and Tony Vallone's Corporate Executive Chef. Ever humble, Bruce credits his success with "using the freshest, best-quality ingredients. If you use the highest quality ingredients available, the flavors will take care of themselves." McMillian's modest philosophy belies his gift for combining flavors and colors, his knack for taking the ordinary and elevating it to the sublime, and a passion for food unequaled by few in the business. "Once cooking gets in your blood, you can't get away from it. That's really how I see it. So even when I'm not in the kitchen or working actively on a dish or on my menu, I'm thinking up new recipes, creating combinations in my mind." Bruce's golden touch has spun such culinary gems as linguine with crab and lobster mushrooms in a Spumante glaze and chilled capellini with scampi and crisp asparagus in lemon essence. "I initially started out thinking I would go to law school, become a high-powered Texas lawyer. Now I cook for the very people I would have been working with instead!" says Bruce with a laugh.

linguine, crab, and lobster mushrooms in spumante reduction
The Asti-laced beurre blanc for this sumptuous pasta is scented with shallots and fresh sage, underscoring the sweetness of the crab.

Bring 5 quarts of water to a boil, add the linguine and salt, and cook until the linguine are al dente. Drain.

Meanwhile, in a heavy saucepan, place the shallots, Spumante, and broth. Bring to a boil over medium heat and reduce to one-fifth of the original volume, about 5 minutes. Whisk in the cream and one-third of the mushrooms, season with salt and pepper, and continue to cook until the sauce has become thick, almost like a glaze, about 5 more minutes. Whisk in all but 3 teaspoons of the butter by the tablespoon; the sauce should become thick. Add the sage, and remove the sauce from the heat. Fold the remaining mushrooms, the remaining butter, and the crab into the sauce. If necessary, adjust the seasoning.

In a large serving bowl, toss the linguine with the sauce, and serve immediately.

serves 4

1 pound linguine
salt
12 shallots, minced
1 cup Asti Spumante
1 cup chicken broth (see page 183)
2 cups heavy cream
12 ounces lobster mushrooms, scrubbed and sliced
freshly ground black pepper
2 1/2 sticks (20 tablespoons) unsalted butter, cubed
3 sage leaves, chopped
1 pound cooked jumbo lump crabmeat, picked over

chilled **capellini**, scampi, and asparagus in a zesty lemon essence

Bruce prefers to use only the pretty asparagus tips in this stunning dish, and reserves the stalks for soups or risottos.

serves 4

1 pound scampi
24 pencil-thin asparagus spears, trimmed
12 ounces capellini
salt
4 lemons
$1/2$ cup extra-virgin olive oil
$1/4$ cup champagne vinegar
freshly ground black pepper
$1 1/2$ tablespoons chopped Italian parsley
$1/8$ teaspoon chili flakes (optional)

Bring 5 quarts of water to a boil, and drop in the scampi. Cook for 5 minutes, then remove with a slotted spoon, reserving the boiling water. Cool the scampi, then shell the tails and cut the tail meat into 2 medallions.

Drop the asparagus into the reserved boiling water, and cook for 30 seconds; remove with a slotted spoon to a bowl of cold water (once again, reserving the pot of boiling water), drain, and cut into $1 1/2$" pieces.

Drop the capellini and salt into the boiling water, and cook until al dente. Drain and spread out on a large tray to cool.

Meanwhile, grate the zest of 2 of the lemons; place in a bowl with the olive oil and vinegar. Squeeze all 4 lemons, and pour the lemon juice into the bowl. Season with salt and pepper. Toss the capellini with half of the vinaigrette in the bowl. Stir in the parsley and chili. Pile the capellini in a large platter. Toss the scampi and asparagus with the remaining vinaigrette, and arrange over the pasta. Serve within 30 minutes.

fettuccelle and baby octopus in lemon-basil pesto

Baby octopus have a much more tender texture than large ones, and look mighty adorable sitting atop a mound of fettuccelle.

Heat a small skillet over medium heat. Add the pine nuts and cook, stirring constantly, until toasted all over, about 3 minutes. Place the pine nuts, peeled garlic cloves, and basil in the bowl of a food processor; process until a coarse paste forms. With the motor running, work in 1 cup of the olive oil until smooth; turn out into a bowl and stir in the Parmigiano with a fork. Add salt and set aside.

In a large skillet over medium heat, heat the remaining olive oil and cook the minced garlic for 30 seconds. Add the octopus, season with salt and pepper, and cook 30 seconds, or until the octopus curl up. Deglaze with the wine; cook 7 minutes. Add the chili, remove from the heat, and fold in 1 cup of the pesto and the lemon zest.

Meanwhile, bring 5 quarts of water to a boil. Add the fettuccelle and salt, and cook until al dente. Drain. Return the fettuccelle to the pot, stir in the remaining pesto, turn into a serving bowl, and top with the octopus. Adjust the seasoning and serve hot.

serves 4

1 tablespoon pine nuts
4 garlic cloves, 2 peeled and 2 minced
4 bunches basil, leaves only
1 cup plus 3 tablespoons extra-virgin olive oil
$1/2$ cup freshly grated Parmigiano Reggiano
salt
2 pounds baby octopus, rinsed
freshly ground black pepper
$1/2$ cup dry white wine
1 teaspoon chili flakes
1 teaspoon grated lemon zest
1 pound fettuccelle

orecchiette with rabbit, broccoli raab, shaved garlic, and porcini

The rabbit for the sauce can be braised up to 24 hours ahead and refrigerated until needed, covered by its braising liquid.

Heat 2 tablespoons of the olive oil in a skillet and add the onion, carrot, celery, bay leaf, parsley, and thyme; cook for 10 minutes over medium heat, stirring often. Stir in the rabbit, and cook 10 more minutes, or until browned all over, turning once. Deglaze with the wine; when it evaporates, after about 3 minutes, pour in 2 cups of water and bring to a boil. Lower the heat to medium-low; cook, covered, for 1 hour, or until the rabbit is fork-tender. Remove the rabbit to a plate, shred it, and season with salt and pepper; strain the liquid, discarding the solids, and set aside.

Meanwhile, bring 5 quarts of water to a boil. Drop in the broccoli raab and salt, and cook 5 minutes; remove to a bowl of cold water with a slotted spoon (reserving the pot of boiling water), then drain and chop.

Heat the remaining olive oil in a skillet large enough to accommodate the orecchiette later. Add the garlic, and cook for 30 seconds. Fold in the broccoli raab and shredded rabbit without the reserved liquid, and cook for 5 minutes.

Add the orecchiette and salt to the reserved boiling water, and cook until al dente. Drain, reserving 2 tablespoons of the pasta cooking water.

Add the reserved pasta cooking water to the rabbit sauce, season with salt, pepper, and the crushed red pepper, and stir in the porcini. Cook for 1 minute. Pour in 1 cup of the reserved rabbit braising liquid, bring to a boil, and stir in the orecchiette. Adjust the seasoning if needed, and serve hot.

serves 4

1/2 cup extra-virgin olive oil
1 onion, minced
1 carrot, minced
1 celery stalk, minced
1 bay leaf
2 Italian parsley sprigs
1 thyme sprig
1 boneless rabbit loin
1/2 cup dry white wine
salt and freshly ground black pepper
1 bunch broccoli raab, tough stems and yellow leaves removed
10 garlic cloves, thinly sliced
1 pound orecchiette
1/2 teaspoon crushed red pepper
8 ounces porcini mushrooms, scrubbed and sliced 1/4" thick

rigatoni with roasted red and yellow peppers, sausage, and barolo
The ridges in the rigatoni grab onto the hearty sausage and roasted pepper sauce; penne rigate, conchiglie rigate, or gemelli would also be ideal pastas, says Bruce.

Preheat the broiler: Cut the red and yellow peppers in half, remove the seeds and stems, and place on an aluminum foil-lined baking sheet. Broil until charred all over, turning 2 or 3 times, about 20 minutes. Remove from the oven, wrap in the foil, and set aside to cool to room temperature. Unwrap the peppers, slip off the skins, and dice. Set aside.

Heat 2 tablespoons of the olive oil in a skillet large enough to hold the rigatoni later and add the sausage. Sauté over medium heat until the sausage is cooked through, about 10 minutes. Discard the fat in the skillet. Add the remaining olive oil and the garlic, and cook for 30 seconds.

Fold in the diced roasted peppers, deglaze with the Barolo, and cook over medium heat for 3 minutes, or until the Barolo has nearly evaporated. Add the tomato sauce, salt, pepper, and basil, and cook until heated through, about 2 minutes, stirring.

Meanwhile, bring 5 quarts of water to a boil. Add the rigatoni and salt, and cook until al dente. Drain. Toss the rigatoni with the sauce, adjust the seasoning, and turn out into a heated serving bowl. Top with the ricotta salata, and serve hot.

serves 4

1 red pepper
1 yellow pepper
$1/3$ cup extra-virgin olive oil
1 pound Italian sausage,
   casings removed and crumbled
4 garlic cloves, chopped
$1/2$ cup Barolo
1 cup tomato sauce (see page 185)
salt and freshly ground black pepper
24 basil leaves, torn
1 pound rigatoni
1 cup freshly grated ricotta salata
   or Pecorino Romano

umberto **menghi**

tagliolini in roasted seafood ragù •
fettuccine in creamy veal and asparagus
sauce • penne with cauliflower florets
and olives • fusilli rigati in spicy
broccoli cream • linguine and string
beans in lemon sauce

"**When I was** a boy, my parents wanted me to become a priest. I grew up on a farm in Tuscany, and being a priest was a noble path in most people's eyes. But that's not what I wanted. So when I was twelve, I ran away from home, and took shelter in a restaurant in the countryside. My father found me, and I begged him to let me stay at the restaurant and earn my living there. Three years later, I convinced my parents—who still wanted me to become a priest!—to let me attend hotel management school. I thought that would be my ticket to travel the world, and in a way it was," says Umberto Menghi, noted Canadian television cooking personality, cookbook author, and owner of a cooking school in Tuscany and eight Italian restaurants in Vancouver, including the famed Umberto's. After graduating from school in Rome, Umberto worked at the Hilton and the Savoy in London, then made his way to Montreal, where he worked at the Queen Elizabeth Hotel. A friend convinced him to head West, and off Umberto went to conquer Canada's Wild West. Thirty years later, Umberto remains a pioneer on the Canadian culinary scene. He was the first to offer authentic Tuscan cuisine in Vancouver, the first to break the "spaghetti and meatballs" stereotype. His cooking style stresses simplicity above all, and his favorite dishes remain those he grew up enjoying on his farm in Tuscany: "When I'm tired or out of sorts, just give me a portion of pappardelle in duck sauce. Despite all my world travels," he jokes, "I'm still a Tuscan at heart."

tagliolini in roasted seafood ragù

Always striving for intense flavor, Umberto roasts mussels, clams, sea bass, and shrimp with herbs and wine before tossing them into the skillet.

serves 4

8 mussels
10 clams
salt
14 ounces boneless, skinless sea bass filet
4 medium shrimp, shells on
1 rosemary sprig
4 sage leaves
$1/4$ cup dry white wine
freshly ground black pepper
$1/4$ cup extra-virgin olive oil
2 garlic cloves, coarsely chopped
4 plum tomatoes, peeled, seeded, and cubed
1 leek, white part only, thinly sliced
2 tablespoons minced Italian parsley
$1/4$ teaspoon spicy olive oil
1 pound tagliolini

Scrub the mussels, pulling off any beards. Rinse the mussels and clams, and place in a bowl; cover with cold water; add 1 tablespoon of salt, and soak for 30 minutes. Drain and rinse. Preheat the oven to 375°. In a large baking dish, combine the sea bass, shrimp, mussels, clams, rosemary, sage, wine, salt, and pepper. Add $1/2$ cup of cold water, and bake for 8 minutes, or until the clams and mussels open; discard any unopened clams or mussels. Remove the baking dish from the oven and allow the fish and seafood to cool. Shell the shrimp, clams, and mussels. Discard the shells. Coarsely chop all the fish and shellfish. Strain the cooking juices through a filter-lined sieve into a bowl, and add to the fish and shellfish.

In a sauté pan large enough to hold the tagliolini later, heat the olive oil. Add the garlic and cook until golden, about 30 seconds. Stir in the tomatoes, leek, parsley, and spicy olive oil, and cook for 8 minutes over medium heat. Fold in the fish and shellfish, the reserved cooking juices, salt, and pepper. Cover the pan, and simmer 5 minutes.

Meanwhile, bring 5 quarts of water to a boil. Add the tagliolini and salt; cook until al dente. Drain; toss with the seafood sauce in the pan, adjust the salt, and serve hot.

fettuccine in creamy veal and asparagus sauce

Umberto uses fresh ricotta instead of heavy cream to give a creamy quality to this elegant pasta. Don't bring the sauce to a boil once you add the ricotta, or it might curdle.

Trim the asparagus, removing the tough lower portion of each spear. Bring 5 quarts of water to a boil and add the asparagus spears; cook for 2 minutes, then remove with a slotted spoon to a bowl of cold water. Drain and cut the asparagus into 1" pieces. Reserve the boiling water.

Season the veal loin with salt and pepper. In a skillet, heat 3 tablespoons of the olive oil and brown the veal on both sides, turning once; it will take about 5 minutes. Remove to a plate, cool, cut into $1/2$"-thick slices, and cube; set aside.

In a medium skillet, combine the butter, the remaining olive oil, and the shallots, and cook over medium heat until the shallots are translucent, about 1 minute. Stir in the cubed veal, the asparagus, and the ricotta. Pour in the broth, and cook for 2 minutes.

Meanwhile, drop the fettuccine and salt into the reserved boiling water; cook until al dente, and drain.

Transfer the fettuccine to a large serving bowl, and fold in the asparagus and veal sauce. Adjust the salt and pepper if needed, sprinkle with the parsley, and serve hot, garnished with the Parmigiano.

serves 4

12 pencil-thin asparagus spears
8 ounces veal loin
salt and freshly ground black pepper
$1/4$ cup extra-virgin olive oil
2 tablespoons unsalted butter
4 shallots, thinly sliced
$1/4$ cup fresh ricotta
$1/4$ cup chicken broth (see page 183)
8 ounces fettuccine
1 teaspoon finely chopped Italian parsley
$1/4$ cup freshly grated Parmigiano Reggiano (optional)

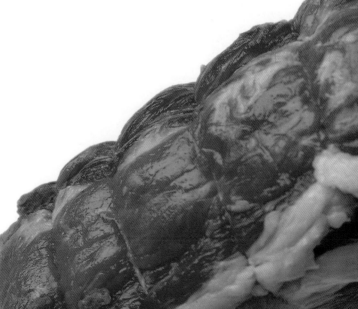

penne with cauliflower florets and olives

Humble cauliflower is elegantly transformed in this dish, thanks to the striking contrast between the white cauliflower, black olives, and green basil in the anchovy-laced sauce.

Bring 5 quarts of water to a boil. Add the cauliflower florets and salt, and cook for 5 minutes, or until the stems can easily be pierced with a knife; remove with a slotted spoon to a bowl of cool water, and set aside. (Reserve the pot of boiling water.)

Add the penne to the pot of boiling water, and cook until al dente; drain.

Meanwhile, in a skillet large enough to hold the penne later, heat the olive oil. Add the drained cauliflower florets, olives, and anchovies, and cook over medium heat for 5 minutes, stirring often; the anchovies should have melted into the oil, and the cauliflower should be shiny all over.

Fold the penne into the sauce in the skillet, and cook for 1 minute, adjusting the salt and adding pepper as needed. Sprinkle with the Pecorino, and spoon onto 4 heated plates. Garnish with the basil, and serve hot.

serves 4

1 head cauliflower, cut into florets
salt
1 pound penne
$1/4$ cup extra-virgin olive oil
$1/2$ cup Kalamata olives,
    pitted and finely chopped
7 anchovy filets, rinsed and chopped
freshly ground black pepper
$1/2$ cup freshly grated Pecorino Romano
12 basil leaves, torn

fusilli rigati in spicy broccoli cream

Umberto's secret: he adds arugula, pine nuts, and lemon zest to his creamy broccoli sauce, elevating the flavors from the savory to the sublime.

serves 4

1 head broccoli, cut into florets
2 shallots, chopped
$1/4$ cup dry white wine
$1/8$ teaspoon crushed red pepper
2 tablespoons extra-virgin olive oil
$1/4$ cup pine nuts
1 bunch arugula, washed, stems removed
$1/4$ cup heavy cream
grated zest of $1/4$ lemon
salt and freshly ground black pepper
1 pound fusilli rigati
$1/2$ cup freshly grated Pecorino Romano
    or Parmigiano Reggiano

Place the broccoli, shallots, wine, crushed red pepper, and 1 cup of water in a saucepan; cover, and cook over medium heat until the broccoli is soft, about 10 minutes. Transfer the solids and liquid to a food processor, and purée until smooth; alternately, you can pass the mixture through a food mill fitted with a medium disk, discarding the solid bits that stick to the disk of the food mill.

In a clean skillet large enough to hold the fusilli rigati later, heat 1 tablespoon of the olive oil. Add the pine nuts and cook over medium heat, stirring, for 2 minutes, or until golden; remove to a plate. Add the remaining olive oil to the skillet, and stir in the arugula. Cook for 3 minutes, or until wilted; add the puréed broccoli, cream, lemon zest, pine nuts, salt, and pepper, and cook over medium-low heat for 4 minutes.

Meanwhile, bring 5 quarts of water to a boil. Add the fusilli rigati and salt, and cook until al dente; drain. Toss the fusilli rigati into the skillet with the broccoli sauce, adjust the salt, and sauté for 1 minute. Transfer to a heated serving bowl. Serve hot, topped with the Pecorino or Parmigiano.

linguine and string beans in lemon sauce

Another lean and delicious dish from Umberto. This time, Umberto uses yogurt to lend creaminess, but not too many calories, to the sauce.

Bring 5 quarts of water to a boil and add the string beans. Cook for 2 minutes; remove with a slotted spoon to a bowl of ice water to set the color and stop the cooking, and drain (reserve the pot of boiling water). Cut the drained string beans into 1" pieces and set aside.

Add the linguine and salt to the pot of boiling water, and cook until al dente; drain, reserving 1/2 cup of the pasta cooking water.

Meanwhile, in a sauté pan large enough to accommodate the linguine later, combine the yogurt, lemon zest, string beans, and butter. Set over medium heat and cook for 5 minutes, or until the sauce is warm; be careful not to bring the sauce to a boil, or the yogurt might curdle.

Fold the linguine into the sauce. Toss gently, adding a little of the reserved pasta cooking water to dilute the sauce, and fold in the Parmigiano. Adjust the salt, season with the pepper, and spoon into 4 plates. Sprinkle the linguine with the chives and mint, and serve immediately.

serves 4

8 ounces string beans, tipped
1 pound linguine
salt
1/2 cup plain whole-milk yogurt
grated zest of 1 lemon
1 tablespoon unsalted butter
1/2 cup freshly grated Parmigiano
    Reggiano
freshly ground black pepper
1 tablespoon snipped chives
1 tablespoon finely chopped mint

tagliatelle and veal pasticcio •
pappardelle in hare sauce • buckwheat
pizzoccheri with cabbage, potatoes,
and fontina • spaghetti with tomato,
bacon, and marjoram • turkey-stuffed
rigatoni with bubbling gruyère

walter
potenza

Walter Potenza redefines the self-made chef. Executive Chef and owner of Walter's La Locanda del Coccio and Aqua Viva EuroBistro in Providence, Rhode Island and the Sunflower Café in Cranston, Rhode Island, Walter also runs two cooking schools, has an online business promoting his signature clay-pot cookery, recently wrote a book, is the President of ItalCuochi for North America, just opened a shop called Etruria (where he sells, among other things, claypot cookware), and has won an Emmy for his televised cooking show—not bad for someone who never went to cooking school. Walter fell in love with cooking in 1972, and in 1985, his first restaurant, Walter's, was born. Ten years later, he opened Walter's La Locanda del Coccio, where he serves the food of his native Abruzzo as well as Jewish-Italian dishes and clay-pot specialties. "I have never created a dish in my life," says Walter. "The highest respect we can pay a cuisine is to make a step forward by going back in time. You can't simply recreate Italian cuisine because you feel like it. If it's been done a certain way for three thousand years, who am I to change it?" And so Walter continues to bake tagliatelle just like his grandmother used to do in Abruzzo, insisting that the secret to his success isn't training: "It's tradition."

tagliatelle and veal pasticcio

In Italian, pasticcio means mess. But in culinary terms, it refers to dishes in which ingredients are layered together and then baked, such as this tagliatelle creation.

Preheat the oven to 350°. Heat the olive oil in a heavy pan, and add the onion, carrot, celery, and garlic. Cook over medium heat for 7 minutes, or until the vegetables are aromatic and soft, stirring often.

Fold in the tomatoes, veal, chicken livers, salt, and pepper. Cover the pan, lower the heat to medium-low, and simmer for 30 minutes.

Meanwhile, bring 5 quarts of water to a boil. Add the tagliatelle and salt, and cook until al dente. Drain thoroughly.

Butter a large oven-to-table baking dish. Spread one-third of the tagliatelle over the bottom of the baking dish, sprinkle with one-third of the veal sauce, and cover with one-third of the egg slices and the mozzarella. Continue layering the ingredients until they are all used up; you should have 3 layers in all. Sprinkle the Pecorino on top of the final layer. Bake for 20 minutes, or until golden brown. Serve immediately.

serves 6

7 tablespoons extra-virgin olive oil
1 onion, chopped
1 carrot, chopped
1 celery stalk, chopped
1 garlic clove, thinly sliced
3 1/2 cups canned strained plum tomatoes
12 ounces ground veal
6 ounces ground chicken livers
salt and freshly ground black pepper
10 ounces tagliatelle,
    broken into 2" lengths
1 tablespoon unsalted butter for greasing
2 hard-boiled eggs, sliced
4 ounces mozzarella, cut into strips
1/4 cup freshly grated Pecorino Romano

pappardelle in hare sauce

You can substitute rabbit for the hare if the hare is hard to find, but the dish will have a less gamy flavor as a result.

serves 4

1 hare, cleaned and cut into 1" pieces
2$^1/_4$ cups dry red wine
1 celery stalk, chopped
1 onion, sliced
1 bay leaf
$^1/_2$ teaspoon black peppercorns
3 ounces fatty pork
1 carrot
$^1/_4$ cup extra-virgin olive oil
salt and freshly ground black pepper
$^1/_2$ cup beef broth (see page 183)
1 pound pappardelle
$^3/_4$ cup freshly grated Parmigiano
   Reggiano
4 tablespoons unsalted butter,
   room temperature

Place the hare pieces in a bowl and add the wine, celery, half of the onion, the bay leaf, and the peppercorns. Toss well to coat, and allow it to marinate for 4 hours in the refrigerator, stirring from time to time to distribute the flavors.

Mince the fatty pork with the remaining onion and the carrot in a meat grinder; you can also do this with a sharp knife. Heat the olive oil in a large, heavy pan, add the ground pork mixture, and cook, stirring, over medium heat for 5 minutes, or until the pork has changed color.

Drain the hare from the marinade (reserve the marinade), and add it to the pan. Season with salt and pepper. Sear until brown on all sides, turning to cook evenly, then add one-quarter of the reserved marinade and all of the broth. Bring to a gentle boil; cover, and cook for about 1$^1/_2$ hours, or until the hare is tender, stirring occasionally and adding more of the marinade if needed to keep the sauce from drying out. Transfer the pieces of hare to a warmed serving dish. Strain the cooking juices, discarding the solids, and keep hot.

Meanwhile, bring 5 quarts of water to a boil. Add the pappardelle and salt, and cook until al dente. Drain. Toss the pappardelle gently with the hare in the serving dish, and moisten with the cooking juices as needed. Fold in the Parmigiano and the butter, adjust the salt if necessary, and serve immediately.

buckwheat **pizzoccheri** with cabbage, potatoes, and fontina A traditional dish in the Valtellina area of Lombardy. Use Fontina from Val d'Aosta if Bitto is unavailable in your cheese shop.

Bring 6 quarts of water to a boil in a large pot. Drop in the potatoes and cabbage, and cook for 15 minutes. Add the pizzoccheri and salt, and cook until the pizzoccheri are al dente. Drain.

Meanwhile, melt the butter in a small pan with the garlic and sage. Cook over medium heat until the garlic is golden and the sage has let off its aroma, about 30 seconds. Remove the garlic and sage from the butter.

Spoon half of the pizzoccheri into a large, heated (preferably terra-cotta) serving dish. Pour on half of the butter, then scatter half of the Bitto or Fontina over the pizzoccheri and season with a generous amount of pepper. Make a second layer with the remaining pizzoccheri, butter, and Bitto or Fontina, and sprinkle the top with more pepper. Serve immediately.

serves 6

2 potatoes, peeled and
   cut into $1/2$" cubes
1 head Savoy cabbage, cored and sliced
   into thin strips
1 pound pizzoccheri
salt
$1 1/2$ sticks (12 tablespoons) unsalted
   butter, cubed
2 garlic cloves, peeled
2 sage leaves
6 ounces Bitto or Fontina from
   Val d'Aosta, cut into $1/2$" cubes
freshly ground black pepper

spaghetti with tomato, bacon, and marjoram

Called spaghetti col rancetto in Abruzzo, this pasta sauce—a variation on Rome's famous amatriciana—relies on fresh marjoram for its unique character. The final flourish of Pecorino Romano ties all the flavors together.

Heat the olive oil in a heavy pan, and add the onion and bacon. Cook over medium heat for 5 minutes, stirring constantly, or until the onion is translucent and the bacon has rendered its fat and become opaque; do not allow the bacon or onion to brown, or the dish will acquire an altogether different character.

Stir in the tomatoes, and cook for 10 more minutes. Add the marjoram, and season with salt and pepper; the sauce should be quite peppery and fragrant from the marjoram. Keep warm.

Meanwhile, bring 5 quarts of water to a boil. Add the spaghetti and salt, and cook until al dente. Drain, then pile into a warmed serving dish.

Pour the hot marjoram-laced tomato sauce over the top, sprinkle with half of the Pecorino, and fold gently to mix. Adjust the salt if needed and serve immediately, topped with the remaining Pecorino.

serves 4

$1/4$ cup extra-virgin olive oil
1 onion, thinly sliced
3 ounces slab bacon, diced
2 cups canned chopped plum tomatoes
1 tablespoon chopped marjoram
salt and freshly ground black pepper
1 pound spaghetti
$1/2$ cup freshly grated Pecorino Romano

turkey-stuffed **rigatoni** with bubbling gruyère

A rustic dish with impressive flavor, typical of the way Walter cooks. Be sure to use freshly grated nutmeg, not the faded, pre-grated powder sold in supermarkets, in the turkey filling.

Preheat the oven to 400°. Grind the turkey, chicken livers, Prosciutto Cotto, and mushrooms together in a meat grinder; alternately, you can use a food processor to do the job, but don't process the ingredients so long that they heat up and become pasty as a result.

Melt 2 tablespoons of the butter in a heavy pan, add the onion, and cook over medium heat until golden. Stir in the ground turkey mixture and cook, stirring, for 10 more minutes. Deglaze with the wine and cook until it has evaporated by half, about 2 minutes; add the nutmeg, and season with salt and pepper. Transfer the mixture to a bowl, and add enough of the cream to achieve a smooth, creamy texture; cool to room temperature.

Meanwhile, bring 4 quarts of water to a boil. Drop in the rigatoni and salt, and cook until al dente. Drain, spread out on a baking sheet to cool, then stuff the rigatoni with the turkey mixture.

Grease a large oven-to-table baking dish with 2 tablespoons of the butter. Arrange the stuffed rigatoni in 2 layers in the baking dish, covering each layer with the remaining cream and sprinkling with the Gruyère. Cube the remaining butter and scatter it over the top; bake for 15 minutes. Serve immediately.

serves 4

6 ounces boneless and skinless turkey breast, chopped
2 chicken livers
4 ounces Prosciutto Cotto, chopped
10 button mushrooms, scrubbed
1 stick (8 tablespoons) unsalted butter
1 small onion, chopped
$1/2$ cup dry white wine
$1/8$ teaspoon freshly grated nutmeg
salt and freshly ground black pepper
1 cup heavy cream
12 ounces rigatoni
3 ounces Gruyère, grated

marcello **russodivito**

pappardelle, zucchini, and speck •
mafaldine with oven-roasted cherry
tomatoes and crab • arugula, shrimp,
and black olive linguine • mezzi
rigatoni with tiny lamb meatballs and
melting scamorza • pennoni with
saffron-laced seafood ragù

When you stop to consider that Marcello Russodivito—owner of two Italian restaurants, one café, and one pizzeria—graduated from the prestigious culinary institute in Montecatini Terme, Tuscany, at the young age of nineteen, it all falls into place. How else could a forty-two-year-old chef have achieved so much in so short a time? Certain that he wanted to be a chef, the young Marcello, a native of Molise, got a head start: he enrolled in cooking school at fourteen, then spent the decade following his graduation traveling the globe to sharpen his culinary prowess. He worked in restaurant kitchens in Switzerland, France, and Bermuda, where he met and fell in love with his wife Carolyn. In 1983, he followed Carolyn to New York, with plans of opening his own Italian restaurant as soon as possible. Within three years, he launched his first restaurant, Marcello's of Suffern, creating a traditional Italian menu for his loyal clientele; among his most requested dishes are sophisticated offerings like Angus beef in a red wine glaze, roasted lamb with rosemary, and chestnut gnocchi in a delicate tomato sauce. Just across the street from Marcello's, Caffè Dolce was born in 1996, home to a tantalizing array of pizzas, sandwiches, and desserts. His latest brainchild is Ho-Ho-Kus, New Jersey's Ho-Ho-Kus Inn. "I tend to like straight-forward, uncomplicated food, and that's what I offer my clients. Squid-ink pasta with clams and shrimp, capellini with crab and roasted tomato. The sort of food I want to eat at home with my wife and kids."

pappardelle, zucchini, and speck
If you can get your hands on zucchini blossoms, throw a few into this summery pasta sauce. Look for them at farmers' markets and specialty greengrocers, or, if you have a garden, grow your own zucchini and keep those gorgeous blossoms for cooking.

In a large pot, bring 5 quarts of water to a boil; add the pappardelle and salt, and cook until al dente. Drain.

In the meantime, heat the olive oil and 3 tablespoons of the butter in a saucepan large enough to hold the pappardelle later. Add the zucchini and Speck, and cook for 1 minute, or until the Speck changes color and the zucchini start to soften around the edges. Stir in the cherry tomatoes and pour in the broth, and bring the liquid in the pan to a boil. Cook for 5 minutes, or until the tomatoes start to break down into a sauce and the broth reduces by about one-third.

Add the pappardelle to the sauce in the pan. Fold in the remaining butter, the grated Parmigiano, and the chives, mixing thoroughly. Adjust the salt if needed, and transfer to a large heated bowl. Serve hot, garnished with the shaved Parmigiano.

serves 4

1 pound pappardelle
salt
2 tablespoons extra-virgin olive oil
6 tablespoons unsalted butter
1 pound baby zucchini, julienned
4 ounces Speck or smoked ham,
   julienned
8 ounces cherry tomatoes
1 cup chicken broth (see page 183)
4 ounces freshly grated Parmigiano
   Reggiano
2 bunches chives, snipped
2 ounces shaved Parmigiano Reggiano

mafaldine with oven-roasted cherry tomatoes and crab

In this Marcello signature dish, cherry tomatoes are coated with a little olive oil, then slowly roasted in a low oven until their skins shrivel and their flesh becomes intensely sweet. Be sure to allow at least 3 hours to cook the tomatoes.

Preheat the oven to 250°. Place the cherry tomatoes on a baking sheet. Drizzle them with 1/4 cup of the olive oil and roast for 3 hours. Remove the cherry tomatoes from the oven and set aside in a bowl.

In a sauté pan large enough to accommodate the mafaldine later, heat 2 tablespoons of the olive oil. Add the garlic and cook until golden, about 30 seconds over medium heat. Pour in the broth, stir in the crab, and delicately fold in the roasted tomatoes; bring the liquid in the pan to a gentle boil and cook for 5 minutes without stirring, or you might break up the tomatoes.

Meanwhile, bring 5 quarts of water to a boil. Add the mafaldine and salt, and cook until al dente. Drain. Toss the mafaldine with the sauce in the pan, fold in the basil and parsley, and adjust the salt if necessary. Turn out into 4 heated bowls, drizzle with the remaining olive oil, and serve immediately.

serves 4

8 ounces cherry tomatoes
1/2 cup extra-virgin olive oil
2 garlic cloves, minced
1 cup chicken broth (see page 183)
1 pound jumbo lump crabmeat,
    picked over
1 pound mafaldine
salt
24 basil leaves, torn
1/4 cup chopped Italian parsley

arugula, shrimp, and black olive **linguine**

Gaeta, a town between Naples and Rome, is home to some of Italy's most delicious table and cooking olives. Small, black, and plump, they are definitely worth seeking out in Italian markets for this pasta sauce, for salads, or simply for nibbling. If you cannot find Gaeta olives, look for oil-cured black olives instead, and choose a variety that is not too bitter.

In a sauté pan large enough to accommodate the linguine later, heat the olive oil over medium heat. Cook the garlic for 30 seconds, or until it becomes lightly golden and aromatic; do not burn the garlic, or it will take on an acrid flavor. Fold in all but 8 of the arugula leaves, then add the rock shrimp and olives, stirring all the while. Cook for 1 minute, or just until the shrimp start to curl up and the arugula wilts. Stir in the tomato sauce, broth, and cream. Bring to a boil; cook for 5 minutes, stirring often. The liquid in the pan should have reduced by one-quarter.

Meanwhile, bring 5 quarts of water to a boil. Add the linguine and salt, and cook until al dente. Drain the linguine, and toss into the sauce in the pan. Adjust the salt if needed, and transfer to a warm serving bowl. Garnish the top with the remaining arugula, cutting it into a fine julienne first, and serve immediately.

serves 4

1/4 cup extra-virgin olive oil
2 garlic cloves, chopped
1 bunch arugula, washed, stems removed
8 ounces rock shrimp,
    shelled and deveined
1/2 cup pitted Gaeta olives
2 cups tomato sauce (see page 185)
1 cup chicken broth (see page 183)
1/4 cup heavy cream
1 pound linguine
salt

mezzi rigatoni with tiny lamb meatballs and melting scamorza
Marcello's native Molise is the inspiration for this robust pasta dish. He often serves the meatball sauce with Abruzzo's famous maccheroni alla chitarra rather than with mezzi rigatoni.

serves 4

3 slices white bread
1 cup whole milk
1 pound ground lamb
2 eggs, beaten to blend
salt and freshly ground black pepper
1 bunch Italian parsley, leaves only, chopped
$1/2$ cup extra-virgin olive oil
2 ounces Prosciutto, diced
1 pound canned chopped plum tomatoes
1 pound mezzi rigatoni
8 ounces scamorza or mozzarella, cut into $1/6$" cubes
$1/2$ cup freshly grated Parmigiano Reggiano

Make the lamb meatballs: Soak the slices of bread in the milk for 5 minutes; squeeze dry. Combine the lamb, eggs, bread, salt, pepper, and parsley in a bowl. Form into small balls. Heat $1/4$ cup of the olive oil in a skillet, and fry the meatballs until they are golden-brown all over, turning often to cook evenly, about 5 minutes over medium heat. Blot dry on a plate lined with paper towels, and set aside.

Heat the remaining olive oil in a sauté pan large enough to hold the mezzi rigatoni later. Add the Prosciutto, and cook for 30 seconds over medium heat. Fold in the tomatoes; cook for 20 minutes. Stir in the meatballs; cook for another 20 minutes.

Meanwhile, bring 5 quarts of water to a boil. Add the mezzi rigatoni and salt, and cook until al dente. Drain. Toss the mezzi rigatoni with the meatball sauce, adjust the seasoning, and spoon into 4 heated bowls. Top each serving with one-quarter of the scamorza or mozzarella, and sprinkle with the Parmigiano. Serve hot.

pennoni with saffron-laced seafood ragù

Saffron is a favorite ingredient in Abruzzese cuisine, thanks to saffron cultivation around the town of L'Aquila. Marcello likes to use saffron in both meat-based and seafood-based sauces, but particularly enjoys its subtle aroma in dishes featuring white fish like monkfish.

Scrub the mussels and pull off any beards that are still clinging. Rinse the clams. Place the clams and mussels in a large bowl, cover with cool water, and add 1 tablespoon of salt; let soak for 30 minutes. Drain, rinse, and place the mussels and clams in a wide pan over medium heat. Cover; cook until the mussels and clams open, about 10 minutes, shaking the pan back and forth every minute or so. Discard any mussels or clams that have not opened and shell the rest; set aside.

Heat the olive oil in a skillet that is large enough to accommodate the pennoni later. Add the garlic and scallions, and cook 1 minute over medium heat, or until the scallions are wilted and aromatic. Fold in the shrimp, monkfish, mussels, clams, and parsley; cook for 1 minute. Pour in the broth, bring to a boil, and add the saffron, stirring to dissolve. Season with salt and pepper, and cook for 10 minutes, or until the liquid in the pan has reduced to one-quarter of its original volume.

Meanwhile, bring 5 quarts of water to a boil. Drop in the pennoni and salt, and cook until al dente. Drain. Stir the pennoni into the seafood sauce in the skillet, adjust the seasoning, and serve hot.

serves 4

16 mussels
16 clams
salt
$1/4$ cup extra-virgin olive oil
2 garlic cloves, chopped
2 bunches scallions, thinly sliced
1 pound rock shrimp,
  shelled and deveined
1 pound boneless and skinless monkfish,
  cut into $1/4$" dice
1 bunch Italian parsley, leaves only,
  chopped
2 cups fish broth (see page 184)
1 teaspoon saffron
freshly ground black pepper
1 pound pennoni

pino
saverino

balsamic vinegar-glazed rigatoni with basil and pecorino • whole wheat spirali in calabrese anchovy-olive sauce • maltagliati with scallops and radicchio • capellini and crab in yellow pepper purée • conchiglie in arugula-ricotta cream

Mention a movie star's name, and it's more than likely that Pino Saverino has cooked for them. His regular clients include Kathleen Turner, Sophia Loren, Liza Minelli, Sylvester Stallone. What draws them in? "It's simple: they want to eat well, they want to keep their weight down, and I help them do that without feeling deprived." As former Executive Chef of Il Ristorante at the Gables Club in Coral Gables, Florida, and current Executive Chef and owner of Pino's Place in Coral Gables, Pino has won a loyal fan base among stars, jet-setters, and ordinary food-loving folks for his light, refreshing cooking style and his ability to turn humble ingredients into gastronomic feasts. Born in Gioia Tauro, Calabria, Pino grew up in Turin and trained in France, where he later opened a restaurant. He visited Miami in 1985, fell in love with the climate and the city, and decided to stay on: "I grew up on Mamma's cooking, eating olive oil, herbs, a little cheese, lots of pasta, some fish. But most of all, I grew up with the four seasons. And that's how I cook in my restaurant."

balsamic vinegar-glazed **rigatoni** with basil and pecorino

Pino's abundant use of basil, balsamic vinegar, and Pecorino make for a heady, bold, unforgettable pasta.

In a skillet that is large enough to hold the rigatoni later, heat 4 tablespoons of the butter with all of the olive oil until the butter melts. Add the garlic, and cook over medium heat until it is lightly golden, about 30 seconds. Stir in the tomatoes and cook for 5 minutes; pour in the vinegar, and cook for 5 more minutes. Season with salt and pepper, and fold in the basil.

Meanwhile, bring 7 quarts of water to a boil. Add the rigatoni and salt, and cook until al dente; drain.

Toss the rigatoni with the sauce in the pan. Fold in the remaining butter and $1/2$ cup of the Pecorino, turn out into a serving bowl, sprinkle with the remaining Pecorino, and serve immediately.

serves 6

1 stick (8 tablespoons) unsalted butter
$1/2$ cup extra-virgin olive oil
3 garlic cloves, finely chopped
1 pound plum tomatoes, cubed
1 cup balsamic vinegar
salt and freshly ground black pepper
1 bunch basil, leaves only, torn
24 ounces rigatoni
1 cup freshly grated Pecorino Romano

whole wheat **spirali** in calabrese anchovy-olive sauce The cherry tomatoes are optional in this dish.

serves 6

1 cup extra-virgin olive oil
15 salted anchovies, rinsed, deboned, and gutted
1 ounce pork rind or pancetta, julienned
6 garlic cloves, minced
1 cup dry red wine
1 cup salted capers, rinsed and chopped
1 cup pitted oil-cured black olives, chopped
2 dried chili peppers, crumbled
8 ounces cherry tomatoes, halved
1 pound whole wheat spirali
salt
1 bunch Italian parsley, leaves only, chopped
1 cup freshly grated Pecorino Romano

Heat the olive oil in a skillet large enough to hold the spirali later. Add the anchovies and pork rind or pancetta, and cook over medium heat until the anchovies dissolve in the oil and the pork rind or pancetta has become translucent, about 2 minutes, stirring.

Add the garlic; when it is golden, after about 1 minute, pour in the wine and add the capers, olives, and chili. Bring the sauce to a boil; fold in the tomatoes and cook for 5 minutes, or until the wine reduces to one-quarter of its original volume.

In the meantime, bring 5 quarts of water to a boil. Add the spirali and salt, and cook until the spirali are al dente. Drain. Toss the spirali into the sauce in the skillet, and fold in the parsley and Pecorino. Adjust the salt if needed, and serve immediately.

maltagliati with scallops and radicchio

An unusual combination that plays the sweetness of scallops off the bitterness of radicchio. When the maltagliati are tossed with the sauce, they take on a gorgeous rosy hue from the radicchio.

Cook the onion in the olive oil until wilted in a sauté pan large enough to accommodate the maltagliati later; it should take about 5 minutes over medium heat. Add the scallops; cook until seared on both sides, turning once, about 2 minutes. Deglaze with the wine, then fold in the radicchio; cook for 3 minutes. Pour in the cream, bring to a boil, and cook for 3 minutes, or until the liquid in the pan reduces and thickens to a good coating consistency. Season with salt and pepper.

Meanwhile, bring 5 quarts of water to a boil. Add the maltagliati and salt, and cook until al dente; drain. Toss the maltagliati into the pan with the radicchio sauce, stir well to mingle the flavors, and adjust the salt if necessary. Turn out into a serving platter, top with the Gruyère, and serve hot.

serves 6

$1/2$ onion, finely chopped
1 cup extra-virgin olive oil
1 pound bay scallops
1 cup dry white wine
2 heads radicchio, julienned
2 cups heavy cream
salt and freshly ground black pepper
1 pound maltagliati
4 ounces Gruyère, shredded

capellini and crab in yellow pepper purée

Pino removes the skin from the yellow peppers before puréeing them for an even more delicate sauce.

In a sauté pan large enough to hold the capellini later, cook the shallots and garlic in the butter over medium heat for 2 minutes, being careful not to burn the butter or the shallots and garlic will turn dark and bitter. Fold in the crab, and cook for 5 minutes, stirring often. Deglaze with the wine, then add the salt, chili, cream, and parsley. Bring to a gentle boil; lower the heat to medium-low, and cook for 1 more minute.

Purée the yellow peppers in a food processor until creamy and smooth; pass the purée through a sieve to get rid of any remaining lumps.

In the meantime, bring 5 quarts of water to a boil, and add the capellini and salt. Cook until the capellini are al dente. Drain the capellini, and toss into the sauce in the pan; fold in yellow pepper purée, adjust the salt if necessary, transfer to a serving platter, and serve immediately.

serves 6

2 shallots, minced
2 garlic cloves, minced
1 stick (8 tablespoons) unsalted butter
1 pound jumbo lump crabmeat,
   picked over
1 cup dry white wine
salt
1 or 2 dried chili peppers, crumbled
1 cup heavy cream
2 tablespoons finely chopped
   Italian parsley
5 yellow peppers, chopped
1 pound capellini

conchiglie in arugula-ricotta cream

Arugula stars in this vibrant pasta: half of it is sautéed with garlic and onion, then puréed with fresh ricotta, and the other half is left raw and folded into the finished dish to provide a fresh note and a pleasant crunch.

In a large sauté pan, heat the olive oil and add the garlic and onion; cook for 1 minute over medium heat, then fold in half of the arugula. Stir constantly in order to help the arugula wilt in the pan. Deglaze with the wine; bring to a boil and cook for 3 minutes, or until the wine nearly evaporates.

Transfer the arugula-onion mixture to a food processor, spoon in the ricotta, and blend until smooth. Turn out into a serving bowl.

In the meantime, bring 7 quarts of water to a boil. Add the conchiglie and salt, and cook until al dente; drain. Stir the conchiglie into the arugula-ricotta purée in the bowl, and add the remaining arugula. Adjust the salt if needed, top with the Parmigiano, and sprinkle with the pepper. Serve hot.

serves 6

$^1/_2$ cup extra-virgin olive oil
2 garlic cloves, chopped
1 onion, chopped
3 bunches arugula, washed, stems removed, and chopped
1 cup dry white wine
1 pound fresh ricotta
24 ounces conchiglie
salt
$^1/_2$ cup freshly grated Parmigiano Reggiano
freshly ground black pepper

patrizio
siddu

maccheroni alla chitarra with braised leeks • country pennette rigate with sage and tomatoes • pappardelle in tomato-thyme sauce • pennoni with sausage, arugula, and balsamic vinegar • fettuccine with clams, cannellini beans, and rosemary

"It's a variety of thyme that grows wild in Tuscany," says Patrizio Siddu, when asked why he named his Manhattan restaurant Pepolino. "I had been dreaming of opening my own restaurant since I was fifteen and first fell in love with cooking, and I wanted the name of my restaurant to reflect my cooking style. I use a lot of herbs in my dishes—usually just one herb in any one dish, to highlight other flavors—and pepolino is my favorite herb." After graduating from culinary school, Florentine-born Patrizio got his hands-on start in the food business cooking for famous Italian designers at fashion shows. Eager to learn more, he worked at Cibreo, one of Florence's most renowned restaurants, under legendary chef and proprietor Fabio Picchi, then moved on to the Michelin one-star Cantina Barbagianni. In 1995, Patrizio hopped on a plane and made New York City his new home. After two and a half years behind the stoves at Manhattan's Savore and a brief stint at Pier 59 Studios at the Chelsea Piers, Patrizio was ready to turn his dream into a reality. In August 1999, he opened the doors of Pepolino, and thrilled guests with his elegant Tuscan cuisine. Signature dishes run the gamut from fettuccine with clams, cannellini, and rosemary to a sumptuous pear-ricotta tart, and Patrizio is always on hand to convert anyone to the benefits of wild thyme.

maccheroni alla chitarra
with braised leeks
Leeks are cooked until they reach an almost creamy consistency with nothing more than butter, olive oil, and vegetable broth, forming a glorious vegetarian sauce for pasta. Don't rush the leeks as they cook: Patrizio suggests you coax their flavor out gently, slowly, lovingly.

In a sauté pan large enough to hold the maccheroni alla chitarra later, heat the butter and $1/3$ cup of the olive oil. Add the leeks, salt, and pepper, and cook over medium-low heat for 20 minutes, or until the leeks are soft and all of the liquid in the pan has evaporated. It is imperative that the leeks do not brown at all, or the dish will change character.

Add the broth to the leeks in the pan, and bring to a gentle boil. Simmer for 10 more minutes, or until the leeks have broken down into a soft mass, being careful not to allow all the liquid in the pan to evaporate.

Meanwhile, bring 5 quarts of water to a boil. Add the maccheroni alla chitarra and salt, and cook until al dente. Drain. Add the maccheroni alla chitarra, $1/2$ cup of the Parmigiano, and the remaining olive oil to the leek sauce in the pan, stir to combine, and adjust the salt if necessary. Transfer to a heated serving dish, top with the remaining Parmigiano, and sprinkle with some freshly ground black pepper. Serve hot.

serves 4

4 tablespoons unsalted butter
1 cup extra-virgin olive oil
8 large leeks, white part only, minced
salt and freshly ground black pepper
$1 1/2$ cups vegetable broth (see page 184)
1 pound maccheroni alla chitarra
1 cup freshly grated Parmigiano Reggiano

country **pennette rigate** with sage and tomatoes

Patrizio uses purple onions for this dish, since they have a more delicate flavor than yellow onions and retain some of their gorgeous color even after cooking.

Heat the olive oil in a skillet large enough to accommodate the pennette rigate later. Add the garlic, onion, sage, pancetta, and chili flakes, and cook until the onion is golden and soft and the pancetta is no longer raw, about 5 minutes over medium heat. Stir in the tomato sauce, and bring to a boil; cook for 10 minutes.

Season with salt and pepper, but don't overdo it on the salt, because the pancetta is already fairly salty.

In the meantime, bring 5 quarts of water to a boil. Add the pennette rigate and salt, and cook until the pennette rigate are al dente. Drain, reserving $1/2$ cup of the pasta cooking water. Fold the pennette rigate into the sauce, tossing well for 1 minute to marry the flavors and adding some of the reserved pasta cooking water if necessary to dilute the sauce. Adjust the salt if needed, transfer to 4 heated bowls, discard the sage leaves, and dust with the Parmigiano. Serve hot.

serves 4

$1/2$ cup extra-virgin olive oil
2 garlic cloves, minced
1 small purple onion, finely chopped
4 sage leaves
3 ounces pancetta, cubed
$1/8$ teaspoon chili flakes
3 cups tomato sauce (see page 185)
salt and freshly ground black pepper
1 pound pennette rigate
1 cup freshly grated Parmigiano Reggiano

pappardelle in tomato-thyme sauce

Don't be fooled by the simplicity of this Tuscan pasta and the relatively few ingredients used to prepare it: this is one amazing dish. Try it and you'll be hooked, especially if you are an avowed lover of fresh thyme like Patrizio.

Melt the butter with the minced thyme over medium heat in a skillet large enough to accommodate the pappardelle later. After 1 minute, add the tomato sauce, and cook for 1 minute, whisking, or until the butter has combined thoroughly with the tomato sauce in the skillet.

In the meantime, bring 5 quarts of water to a boil. Add the pappardelle and salt, and cook until al dente. Drain the pappardelle, reserving 1/2 cup of the pasta cooking water. Toss the pappardelle with the sauce in the skillet for 1 minute, dilute with some of the reserved pasta cooking water if needed, season with salt and pepper, and spoon into 4 heated plates. Serve the pappardelle immediately, garnished with the whole thyme sprigs.

serves 4

4 tablespoons unsalted butter
12 thyme sprigs, 8 minced and 4 whole
   (leaves only)
3 cups tomato sauce (see page 185)
1 pound pappardelle
salt and freshly ground black pepper

pennoni with sausage, arugula, and balsamic vinegar

It may seem like there is a lot of balsamic vinegar in this recipe, but as the sauce cooks down and the flavors mingle, the sharpness and acidity of the vinegar are boiled off, leaving behind only a subtle tang.

In a sauté pan large enough to hold the pennoni later, heat the olive oil. Add the garlic and cook until golden over medium heat, about 30 seconds. Add the sausage and cook, stirring often to cook evenly, until browned on all sides; it should take about 10 minutes. Deglaze the pan with the vinegar, keeping your face away from the pan since the fumes will be strong and might sting your eyes; cook for 3 minutes; the vinegar will reduce to 1 tablespoon and lose its sharp aroma. Stir in the tomato sauce and cook until slightly reduced, about 15 minutes.

In the meantime, bring 5 quarts of water to a boil. Add the pennoni and salt, and cook until al dente. Drain. Fold the pennoni into the sauce in the skillet, season with pepper, stir in half of the arugula and half of the Parmigiano, and sauté for 1 minute. Transfer to a serving bowl, and top with the remaining arugula and Parmigiano. Serve the pennoni immediately.

serves 4

$^1\!/_2$ cup extra-virgin olive oil
4 garlic cloves, minced
1 pound Italian sausage,
    casings removed and crumbled
$^1\!/_2$ cup balsamic vinegar,
    preferably aged 10 years or longer
3 cups tomato sauce (see page 185)
1 pound pennoni
salt and freshly ground black pepper
4 bunches arugula, washed,
    stems removed, and julienned
1 cup freshly grated Parmigiano Reggiano

fettuccine with clams, cannellini beans, and rosemary
Being a traditionalist, Patrizio uses dried beans for this and other dishes. If you are pressed for time, however, he urges you to use canned cannellini beans rather than forgo the pleasures of this subtle pasta.

Rinse the clams, then place in a bowl, cover with cool water, and add 1 tablespoon of salt; set aside to soak for 30 minutes. Drain and rinse. (This step helps purge the clams of impurities and sand.)

Heat ¼ cup of the olive oil in a skillet that is large enough to hold the fettuccine later. Add the garlic and rosemary, and cook for 30 seconds over medium heat. Add the clams; cover, and cook for 1 minute. Remove the cover, and deglaze with the wine; when the wine has evaporated, after about 1 minute, fold in the cannellini beans. Cook for 10 minutes, allowing the beans to absorb the flavors, the clams to open, and the liquid to reduce. Discard any unopened clams, remove the rosemary sprigs, and keep the sauce warm.

In the meantime, bring 5 quarts of water to a boil. Add the fettuccine and salt, and cook until al dente. Drain, and toss into the sauce in the skillet. Sauté for 1 minute, season with pepper, adjust the salt if needed, and transfer to a heated serving bowl. Drizzle with the remaining olive oil and serve hot.

serves 4

1 pound clams
salt
½ cup extra-virgin olive oil
4 garlic cloves, minced
4 rosemary sprigs
1 cup dry white wine
2 cups cooked cannellini beans
1 pound fettuccine
freshly ground black pepper

maccheroni alla chitarra with red mullet • gnocchetti sardi with sheep sausage • whole wheat spaghetti with scallion purée and bottarga • spinach penne with fresh tuna and capers • rigatoni with hare, cocoa, and grappa

stefano **terzi**

"**I was born** in Bergamo, and we have more than our fair share of exceptional restaurants there. Everyone thinks Milan has the best restaurants in Lombardy, but there are some amazing kitchens in Bergamo, let me tell you," enthuses Stefano Terzi, Executive Chef and co-owner of Manhattan's ViceVersa. After culinary school in San Pellegrino, Tuscany, Stefano worked at several restaurants in Milan and Novara, then became Sous Chef of the just-opened Taverna Del Colleoni Dell'Angelo in his hometown. "I knew I wanted to work in the United States, so in 1995 I moved to Beverly Hills and became Sous Chef at Il Cielo. A year later, I was off to New York, to work under Odette Fada at San Domenico. Then I left for Italy, for a year in the kitchen of the two-star San Domenico in Italy. All in all, I took quite a few planes in a short time," recalls Stefano, who opened ViceVersa in 1999 with fellow San Domenico veterans Franco Lazzari and Daniele Kuchera. "We shared a vision of what a restaurant should be, so it was only right that we should pursue our dream together." Today, Stefano has garnered raves for his sleek, traditional-cum-innovative cuisine. Dishes like whole wheat spaghetti with scallion purée and bottarga, maccheroni alla chitarra topped with pan-fried red mullet in tomato sauce, and grilled herb-crusted baby lamb served atop roasted vegetables embody his clean, stream-lined cooking style: "If there's one thing I learned over the years, it's that less is often more."

maccheroni alla chitarra
with red mullet
In Italy, where fish and seafood are a way of life, pasta sauces made with red mullet are often prepared in home and restaurant kitchens. Stefano's version calls for keeping the fish in pretty filets rather than the small chunks more commonly seen.

Clean the red mullets and filet them, being careful to eliminate all of the bones from the filets, and set aside, reserving the heads and bones for the ragù.

In a sauté pan, heat 2 tablespoons of the olive oil over medium heat and add the shallots and garlic; cook for 3 minutes, or until the shallots are soft. Add the heads and bones of the mullets, and sauté for 3 minutes. Deglaze with the wine, and let it nearly evaporate, about 10 minutes; pour in the tomatoes, and cook the sauce for 15 minutes over low heat without stirring, or you might break up the bones too much. Pour through a strainer to remove the heads and bones of the mullet, and to reduce the tomatoes to a purée.

Meanwhile, bring 10 quarts of water to a boil, add the maccheroni alla chitarra and salt, and cook until al dente. Drain.

In another large pan, heat the remaining olive oil and cook the red mullet filets until they are golden on both sides, turning once, about 5 minutes over medium heat.

Pour in the puréed tomato sauce and the parsley, and cook for 2 more minutes, making sure not to break the red mullet filets; you want to serve them whole, draped over the pasta. Pile the maccheroni alla chitarra on a serving platter, top with the red mullet filets and sauce, and serve hot.

serves 8

12 small red mullets (8 ounces each)
$^{1}/_{3}$ cup extra-virgin olive oil
2 shallots, chopped
2 garlic cloves, chopped
2 cups dry white wine
2 cups canned chopped plum tomatoes
2 pounds maccheroni alla chitarra
salt
1 bunch Italian parsley, leaves only, chopped

gnocchetti sardi with sheep sausage

Sheep sausage has a more pronounced flavor than lamb sausage. If you cannot find it, substitute lamb sausage, which is easier to find at butcher and specialty shops.

serves 8

$1/2$ cup extra-virgin olive oil
2 shallots, chopped
1 dried chili pepper, crumbled
1 pound sheep sausage,
    casings removed and crumbled
4 cups dry red wine
2 cups canned strained plum tomatoes
2 bay leaves
salt
2 pounds gnocchetti sardi
$1/2$ cup freshly grated Pecorino Romano

In a medium saucepan, heat all but 2 tablespoons of the olive oil, and add the shallots and chili. Cook over medium heat for 3 minutes. Add the sausage and cook, stirring, until evenly browned all over, about 5 minutes; this step develops a deep flavor base for the sauce. Pour in just enough of the wine to cover the sausage, and turn the heat to high; cook until the wine evaporates, about 20 minutes, scraping the bottom of the pan to dislodge any caramelized bits. Fold in the tomatoes and bay leaves, lower the heat to medium-low, and cook for 1 hour, or until the sauce is nice and thick and the sausage is tender. Season with salt. Discard the bay leaves.

Meanwhile, bring 10 quarts of water to a boil, and add the gnocchetti sardi and salt. Cook until al dente, drain, and return to the pot. Fold in the sauce. Turn out into a heated platter, sprinkle with the Pecorino and the remaining olive oil, and serve hot.

whole wheat **spaghetti** with scallion purée and bottarga

Bottarga is made from pressed salted fish roe, most commonly from tuna but also from grey mullet. Stefano's dish calls for grey mullet bottarga, whose saltiness mingles with the refreshing scallion purée.

Heat all but 2 tablespoons of the olive oil in a pan over medium heat, add the onion, and sauté until it starts to wilt. Add the scallions, and pour in the broth. Bring to a boil, season with salt, and cook until the scallions are soft yet still vibrantly green, about 3 minutes. Remove from the heat, save $^1/_2$ cup of the scallions, and blend the rest to obtain a nice, smooth purée in a food processor.

Meanwhile, bring 10 quarts of water to a boil, add the spaghetti and salt, and cook until al dente; drain. Toss the spaghetti with the scallion purée in the pot in which you cooked the spaghetti; fold in the reserved scallions and the remaining olive oil. Transfer the pasta to a serving dish, and top with the bottarga. Serve hot.

serves 8

$^1/_2$ cup extra-virgin olive oil
1 onion, thinly sliced
1 pound scallions, chopped
1 cup chicken broth (see page 183)
salt
2 pounds whole wheat spaghetti
3 ounces grey mullet bottarga, shaved

spinach **penne** with fresh tuna and capers

In a pinch, you could use tuna packed in olive oil instead of fresh tuna, but Stefano warns that the flavor will be quite different. If you do use canned tuna, don't heat it before adding it to the penne along with the cherry tomato sauce.

Cook the shallot and garlic in all but 3 tablespoons of the olive oil in a large pan until soft and aromatic, about 5 minutes over medium heat. Add the cherry tomatoes, capers, oregano, salt, and pepper; raise the heat to high and cook for 3 more minutes, or until the tomatoes start to break down into a sauce.

In another skillet, cook the tuna in 2 tablespoons of the olive oil until medium-rare, about 2 minutes over medium-high heat; season with salt and pepper. Set aside.

Meanwhile, bring 10 quarts of water to a boil; add the penne and salt, and cook until al dente. Drain, and toss with the tomato sauce in the pan. Fold in the tuna and bread crumbs, and adjust the seasoning if needed. Transfer to a heated serving bowl, drizzle with the remaining olive oil, and serve immediately.

serves 8

1 shallot, chopped
1 garlic clove, chopped
$2/3$ cup extra-virgin olive oil
8 ounces cherry tomatoes, halved
2 tablespoons capers
1 bunch oregano, leaves only, minced
salt and freshly ground black pepper
1 pound skinless fresh tuna,
    cut into $1/8$" cubes
2 pounds spinach penne
1 tablespoon fresh bread crumbs

rigatoni with hare, cocoa, and grappa

Definitely a bold dish, and one Stefano loves for its direct flavors. The grappa gives it a subtle kick, while the cocoa supplies a haunting chocolate note. The perfect choice for an elegant fall dinner party.

Sprinkle the hare with the salt, pepper, and flour in a plate. Heat the olive oil in a large sauté pan and cook the hare until golden on both sides, about 10 minutes over medium heat, turning once; remove to a plate.

In a saucepan, melt the butter and cook the carrot, onion, and bay leaves until the vegetables are aromatic, about 5 minutes over medium heat. Add the browned hare and the wine to the vegetables in the pan, bring to a gentle boil, and simmer until the meat is coming off the bone, about 1 1/2 hours; if needed, add some of the broth to keep the sauce moist.

About 5 minutes before the hare is cooked, take the pot off the flame and stir in the cocoa and grappa. Return to the flame, and cook for 5 more minutes, in order to allow the alcohol in the grappa to evaporate. When the hare is done, remove the hare pieces to a plate and debone them.

Pass the carrot and onion from the sauce through a food mill or process in a food processor to dice coarsely; return to the sauce and discard the bay leaves. Fold in the deboned hare and adjust the seasoning if needed.

Meanwhile, bring 10 quarts of water to a boil, add the rigatoni and salt, and cook until al dente. Drain. Return the rigatoni to the pot.

Toss the sauce into the pot, stir well, and transfer to a heated serving bowl. Sprinkle with the Parmigiano, and serve hot.

serves 8

1 hare, cleaned and cut into 8 pieces
salt and freshly ground black pepper
1 tablespoon flour
1/3 cup extra-virgin olive oil
1 tablespoon unsalted butter
1 carrot, cut into 3 pieces
1 onion, cut into 3 pieces
4 bay leaves
4 cups dry red wine
1 cup chicken broth (see page 183)
2 tablespoons cocoa powder
1/4 cup grappa
2 pounds rigatoni
1/2 cup freshly grated Parmigiano
   Reggiano

basic recipes

chicken broth

Use a whole chicken for the most intense broth; otherwise opt for chicken legs, or a combination of chicken legs and wings. Using only bones will yield a more watery broth.

makes about 2 quarts

2 pounds chicken parts
1 onion, peeled and quartered
1 carrot, chopped
1 celery stalk, chopped
1 leek, green part only, halved and rinsed
2 garlic cloves, crushed
1 bunch Italian parsley, stems included
4 thyme sprigs
2 bay leaves
1 teaspoon black peppercorns

Rinse the chicken parts and place them in a large pot. Add the remaining ingredients and then pour in enough cold water to cover the ingredients by 1".

Set the pot over a medium-high flame, and bring to a gentle boil, skimming the surface often with a slotted spoon to get rid of the scum that rises to the surface. Lower the heat to medium-low, and simmer, uncovered and without stirring, for 6 hours, or until the liquid in the pot has reduced to less than half of its original volume and the meat is falling off the bone.

Pour the contents of the pot into a cheesecloth-lined colander set over a bowl; discard the solids. Let the broth cool to room temperature, then refrigerate until all the fat solidifies, about 12 hours. Discard the thin layer of fat, and transfer to smaller containers. The broth can be refrigerated for up to 5 days, or frozen for up to 2 months.

beef broth

The bones for beef broth need to be blanched in order to get rid of excess blood; if you omit the blanching step, your broth might be cloudy rather than beautifully transparent.

makes about 2 quarts

2 pounds beef bones
1 onion, peeled and quartered
1 carrot, chopped
1 celery stalk, chopped
1 leek, green part only, halved and rinsed
2 garlic cloves, crushed
1 bunch Italian parsley, stems included
4 thyme sprigs
2 bay leaves
1 teaspoon black peppercorns

Rinse the beef bones and place them in a large pot. Add enough cold water to cover the bones, and bring to a boil. Cook for 1 minute, then drain. Return the beef bones to the pot, add the remaining ingredients, and pour in enough cold water to cover the ingredients by 1".

Set the pot over a medium-high flame, and bring to a gentle boil, skimming the surface often with a slotted spoon to get rid of the scum that rises to the surface. Lower the heat to medium-low, and simmer, uncovered and without stirring, for 6 hours, or until the liquid in the pot has reduced to less than half of its original volume.

Pour the contents of the pot into a cheesecloth-lined colander set over a bowl; discard the solids. Let the broth cool to room temperature, then refrigerate until all the fat solidifies, about 12 hours. Discard the thin layer of fat, and transfer to smaller containers. The broth can be refrigerated for up to 5 days, or frozen for up to 2 months.

fish broth

Avoid fatty fish like salmon for fish broth, and use white fish with a relatively delicate flavor instead: turbot, snapper, and bass are good choices. If you have some shrimp, scampi, or lobster shells, drop them in as well.

makes about 2 quarts

2 pounds fish trimmings
1 onion, peeled and quartered
1 celery stalk, chopped
1 leek, green part only, halved and rinsed
2 garlic cloves, crushed
1 bunch Italian parsley, stems included
4 thyme sprigs
1 bay leaf
1 teaspoon black peppercorns
2 cups dry white wine

Rinse the fish trimmings and place them in a large pot. Add the remaining ingredients, and pour in enough cold water to cover the ingredients by 1".

Set the pot over a medium-high flame, and bring to a gentle boil, skimming the surface often with a slotted spoon to get rid of the scum that rises to the surface. Lower the heat to medium-low, and simmer the broth, uncovered and without stirring, for 30 minutes.

Pour the contents of the pot into a cheesecloth-lined colander set over a bowl; discard the solids. Let the broth cool to room temperature, then refrigerate until all the fat solidifies, about 12 hours. Discard the thin layer of fat, and transfer the broth to smaller containers. The fish broth can be refrigerated for up to 3 days, or frozen for up to $1\frac{1}{2}$ months.

vegetable broth

Use only the freshest ingredients to make vegetable broth, adding any mild vegetable of your liking to the recipe below. Avoid strong-tasting vegetables like turnips or cabbage, however, or you won't end up with a good, all-purpose broth.

makes about 2 quarts

1 fennel bulb, quartered,
  stalks and fronds still attached
1 onion, peeled and quartered
1 carrot, chopped
1 celery stalk, chopped
1 leek, halved and rinsed
4 garlic cloves, crushed
1 bunch Italian parsley, stems included
4 thyme sprigs
2 bay leaves
1 teaspoon black peppercorns

Heat the olive oil in a 1½-quart pot. Add the basil and cook for 5 seconds. Pour in the tomatoes, season with salt, and bring to a boil; cook over medium heat, stirring often, for 30 minutes. Adjust the seasoning and cool to room temperature before storing in the refrigerator or freezer. The sauce will keep in the refrigerator for up to 5 days, and in the freezer for up to 2 months.

Variation: You can do what many chefs do—including those who shared their recipes in this book—and cook down some minced onion, celery, carrot, and garlic in olive oil, then add tomatoes, cook for 1 hour over medium heat, and pass through a food mill to yield a smooth, delicate tomato sauce. See page 17 for an additional recipe for tomato sauce.

besciamella

The familiar béchamel sauce, often needed for oven-baked pastas. You can add a pinch of freshly grated nutmeg if you like, but preferably not if you are incorporating this sauce in a dish that includes tomatoes.

makes about 1 quart

1 stick unsalted butter
3/4 cup all-purpose flour
1 quart milk
salt and freshly ground white pepper

Melt the butter in a 1½-quart saucepan with a heavy bottom. Add the flour and stir with a wooden spoon; cook for 3 minutes over medium-low heat to cook the raw taste out of the flour, but be sure you don't allow the flour to take on any color. Meanwhile, heat the milk in another pot until it is nearly boiling.

Pour the hot milk into the butter-flour mixture, beating constantly with a wire whisk to prevent lumps from forming. Bring to a boil; cook over medium heat, whisking often, until the sauce is thick, about 10 minutes. Lower the heat if the sauce sticks to the bottom of the pan. Season with salt and pepper. The besciamella is ready for use.

Cool the besciamella to room temperature before storing it in the refrigerator. If the besciamella thickens in the refrigerator, whisk in a little cold milk to return it to a flowing consistency before using it.

Place all the ingredients in a large pot and pour in enough cold water to cover the ingredients by 1".

Set the pot over a medium-high flame, and bring to a gentle boil. Lower the heat to medium-low, and simmer, uncovered and without stirring, for 1 hour. Pour the contents of the pot into a cheesecloth-lined colander set over a bowl; discard the solids. Let the broth cool to room temperature, then refrigerate; transfer to smaller containers. The vegetable broth can be refrigerated for up to 5 days, or frozen for up to 2 months.

simple **tomato** sauce

This basic recipe calls only for olive oil and basil as flavorings. During the summer months, use fresh plum tomatoes rather than canned tomatoes as we suggest below, for an even fresher, homey flavor.

makes about 1 quart

1/3 cup extra-virgin olive oil
12 basil leaves
5 cups peeled chopped plum tomatoes (canned
   chopped plum tomatoes are fine if fresh
   tomatoes are not in season)
salt

Maurizio Marfoglia's acorn squash stuffed with mezze penne and shrimp (recipe on page 137) is food fit for a feast.

pasta **glossary**

bucatini From buco, meaning "hole", because this long, cylindrical pasta is hollow in the middle; a favorite in Lazio.

cammaroni lisci Short tubes of pasta, without ridges (hence the word lisci, meaning "smooth"), with slightly curving ends; can be replaced by mezze zite (see below).

capellini Literally, the name of this pasta means "fine hair". Capellini are only slightly thicker than capelli d'angelo (angel hair pasta).

cavatelli Short oval pasta with ridges, native to Apulia and common in other Southern Italian regions. Alternate names for cavatelli are cavatieddi and cavateddi.

conchiglie This shell-shaped pasta is a favorite for chunky vegetable sauces, and is usually ridged.

ditalini A short tubular pasta best used in soups, in pasta e fagioli, and similar rustic preparations. Larger versions are called ditali (medium) and ditaloni (large).

eliche Short, spiral-shaped maccheroni; their name, indicative of their shape, means "propellers".

elicoidali Fat, tubular maccheroni with a slight twist and ridges to catch the sauce; also called torciglioni (see below).

farfalle Translated literally, the word means "butterflies", but farfalle are best known as bowtie pasta.

fedelini From the word filo, meaning "string"; fedelini are thin, long noodles only slightly thicker than capellini (see above), usually served in broth.

fettuccelle Like tagliatelle (see below); thin, flat, and long.

fettuccine Long, flat ribbons of pasta much like tagliatelle (see below), sometimes made with eggs; the word fettuccine is preferred in Southern and Central Italy to the more common Northern term, tagliatelle. Fettuccine are often sold in nests.

fregola A semolina pasta typical of Sardinia, sometimes tinted with saffron. It is either boiled and served with sauce, used in soups, or tossed with savory ingredients after boiling and then baked for a few minutes. Fregolone is the larger version of fregola.

fusilli corti Short fusilli, or corkscrew pasta. Fusilli are typical of Southern Italian cuisine, and usually do not have a hole; those that do are called fusilli bucati. Also called spirali (see below).

fusilli rigati Ridged fusilli, typically narrower than fusilli corti (see above) and coiled around themselves less tightly.

garganelli A classic pasta of Romagna, made with egg even in their dried form. The name comes from garganella, derived from the Latin gargala, meaning "trachea", since the tubular shape of garganelli recalls a cannula used to examine the throat.

gemelli Literally, "twins"; this short pasta is among the best for catching sauces, and resembles industrial versions of strozzapreti (see below). It is made by pulling one strand of pasta back over itself and twisting it, making it appear like two twinned strands.

gnocchetti Tiny dried gnocchi, usually ridged to better soak up the sauce. When they are called gnocchetti sardi, they resemble malloreddus (see below), but are rounded at the ends rather than pointy.

gnocchi Better known in their fresh form (most often made with potatoes and flour), gnocchi are also sold dried. They are hollow in their dried form, and most closely resemble conchiglie (see above), or shell-shaped pasta, but are slightly more open and have scalloped edges. Some are ridged, others are not.

gramignone An unusual and hard-to-find pasta from Romagna, slightly larger than gramigna. Most often served in soups, it consists of short, hollow strands of pasta that are curled over themselves in loose coils.

lasagne Wide, thin sheets of pasta, either with curled or straight edges, perfect for layering with ragùs and rich sauces. Regional variations of lasagne are pappardelle (narrower, from Tuscany; see below); lagane (shorter and narrower, from Apulia and Basilicata); and sagne (from Calabria). Lasagnette are slightly less wide than lasagne.

linguine Native to Liguria, this pasta (literally, "little tongues") is thin, flat, and long; it is sometimes called bavette and lingue di passero.

maccheroni alla chitarra Also called spaghetti alla chitarra, this pasta owes its lyrical name to the stringed instrument, conceived in the Abruzzese town of Chieti, with which it is cut. While it is most common in Abruzzo, it is also enjoyed in nearby Molise.

mafaldine Long, wide noodles with one scalloped edge.

malloreddus Sometimes called Sardinian gnocchi or gnocchetti sardi (see gnocchetti, above), these gnocchi are often colored and flavored with a touch of saffron. Their ends are pointed, and their surface ridged to better catch the sauce.

maltagliati Literally, "badly cut"; this pasta is native to Emilia-Romagna and cut into irregular lozenges. It was born as a way of using up leftover scraps of fresh pasta dough. Penne-like tubes of pasta are sometimes called maltagliati as well.

mezze maniche Translated literally, the name signifies "short sleeves", because of this pasta's short, stubby shape. Mezze maniche look like rigatoni (see below), only slightly wider and half as long. Mezze maniche are not always ridged.

mezze penne "Half penne" (see below). Sometimes ridged, sometimes smooth, they are ideal in soups or for stuffing.

mezze zite The short version of zite (see below), a hollow, tubular, smooth pasta from Campania.

mezzi rigatoni Much like mezze maniche (see above), but slightly less wide and always ridged (rigatoni means "ridged"; see below).

mezzi tubetti Close to ditalini (see above) in their appearance, but slightly curved, these smooth "half tubes" are ideal in soups and broths. They are also good for baked pastas.

orecchiette Shaped like little ears, hence their name; a classic in Apulia and other Southern Italian regions.

orecchini Literally, "earrings", this pasta also goes by the name dischi volanti, meaning "flying saucers".

pappardelle Thin, flat, and long noodles much loved in Tuscany. Dried pappardelle vary in width: some are as narrow as $1/3$", others as wide as $1\,1/2$". Pappardelle are perfect with game sauces.

penne One of the most widely used short pastas, shaped like old pens. Penne are not ridged unless the package specifies otherwise; their diagonally cut ends are excellent for picking up sauces

both dense and light.

pennette Short penne (see above), smooth rather than ridged.

pennette rigate Short penne (see above), ridged.

pennoni Large penne (see above), with the diagonally cut ends characteristic of penne. Most often, they are not ridged; when they are, they are called pennoni rigati.

pizzoccheri Short buckwheat pasta ribbons, a specialty of the Valtellina area of Lombardy, usually served layered with Savoy cabbage, potatoes, and cheese.

rigatoni Wide, tubular pasta about 2" in length, with straight-cut rather than diagonally cut ends, always ridged.

sedanini Medium, tubular pasta, slightly curved and usually ridged.

spaghetti Among the most famous of pasta shapes, spaghetti owe their name to the word spago, meaning "string", because that is what they most closely resemble. Cylindrical and long, they are sometimes called vermicelli (meaning "little worms") in Campania, although vermicelli are slightly thicker.

spaghettini Thin spaghetti, slightly thicker than capellini (see above).

strozzapreti The name means "priest stranglers" in Italy. The dried pasta looks very much like gemelli (see above), while the fresh usually resembles gnocchi (either flour-based or ricotta- and Swiss chard-based, with the latter being much more delicate in texture than the former).

tagliatelle Flat, wide, long ribbons of pasta, often made with egg or spinach, and sometimes sold twirled in nests rather than flat. The name is derived from the verb tagliare, meaning "to cut".

tagliolini Very fine, long pasta, flat rather than cylindrical, indigenous to Northern Italy. It is also called taglierini and tagliatini.

torciglioni Also called elicoidali (see above), this short, wide, tubular pasta has ridges that run diagonally to its axis and straight-cut ends like rigatoni (see above).

trenette Slightly wider than linguine (see above), this pasta is thin, flat, and long.

trofie Tiny twirled gnocchi made with semolina flour and water in Liguria, specifically in the town of Recco, and most often served with basil pesto.

spirali Literally, "spirals", thanks to their spiral-like shape. Spirali are similar to fusilli (see above), but are usually short.

zite Much wider than bucatini (see above), this long, cylindrical, hollow pasta from Campania is sometimes broken into short lengths before being boiled.

zitoni Indigenous to Campania, these hollow, cylindrical, long noodles are the extra-wide version of zite (see above).

mail-order **sources**

AGATA & VALENTINA
1505 1st Avenue
New York, NY 10021
(212) 452-0690
Fine Italian foods imported from Italy, ranging from coffee to olive oils, vinegars, pastas, cheeses, and more.

WWW.ALIMENTITALIA.COM
Fine imported pastas, sauces, olive oils, cheeses, and more.

ALTOMONTE'S ITALIAN MARKET & DELI
85 York Road
Warminster, PA 18974
(215) 672-5439
Gourmet products.

BALDUCCI'S
424 Avenue of the Americas
New York, NY 10011
(800) 225-3822
www.balducci.com
Excellent selection of fresh and dried pastas, cheeses, cured meats, specialty meats and fish, and more.

BUONITALIA
75 9th Avenue
New York, NY 10011
(212) 633-9090
Fresh, dried, and frozen pastas (pizzoccheri, trofie, malloreddus, fregola, garganelli, gramignone, cavatelli, and more), cheeses, olive oils.

CITARELLA
2135 Broadway
New York, NY 10023
(212) 784-0383
Specialty stores selling fresh and dried pastas, fine imported cheeses, meats, fish, seafood, produce, and more.

DEAN & DELUCA
121 Prince Street
New York, NY 10012
(212) 254-8776
www.deandeluca.com
A great selection of dried pastas, olive oil, vinegars, dried beans, cheeses, dried porcini mushrooms, and many other products.

DELVERDE USA, INC.
1901 Research Blvd., Suite 160
Rockville, MD 20850
(800) 222-4409
www.delverde.com
Over 50 varieties of pastas to choose from (including hard-to-find garganelli and pappardelle), olive oil, and other products.

DIBRUNO BROTHERS HOUSE OF CHEESE
930 South 9th Street
Philadelphia, PA 19147
(215) 922-2876
www.dibruno.com
Great selection of imported Italian cheeses, olive oils, cured meats, and much more.

DI PASQUALE MARKETPLACE
3700 Gough Street
Baltimore, MD 21208
(410) 276-6787
Imported foods, wines, gifts, homemade mozzarella, and sausages.

WWW.ESPERYA.COM
A variety of Italian food imports and wines.

ESPOSITO'S PORK SHOP
500 9th Avenue
New York, NY 10018
(212) 279-3298
Italian and specialty meats, and sausages both fresh and imported.

FORMAGGIO KITCHEN
244 Huron Avenue
Cambridge, MA 02138
(888) 212-3224
Cured meats, sauces, olive oils, balsamic vinegars, and more.

GRACE'S MARKET PLACE
1237 3rd Avenue
New York, NY 10021
(212) 737-0600
Fresh and dried pastas, cheeses, produce, olive oil, vinegars, etc.

WWW.ITALIANCULINARY.COM
The finest exclusive estate-bottled extra-virgin olive oils from Italy.

JOE'S ITALIAN MARKET PLACE
2020 Route 9
Lawrence Farms Plaza
Fishkill, NY 12524
(914) 297-1100
www.joesmarketplace.com
Truffle oils, balsamic vinegars, cured meats, mozzarella, and pasta.

KALUSTYAN'S
123 Lexington Avenue
New York, NY 10016
(212) 685-3451
Exotic spices and herbs, breads, grains, dried beans, and more.

MELISSA'S WORLD VARIETY PRODUCE
P.O. Box 21127
Los Angeles, CA 90021
(800) 588-1281
A world of produce delivered to your door.

WWW.PASTACHEESE.COM
Pastas, stuffed pastas, cheeses, olive oils, mozzarella di bufala, balsamic vinegars, all on the internet.

PENSEYS, LIMITED, SPICES AND SEASONINGS
P.O. Box 933
Muskego, WI 53150
(414) 574-0277
Herbs, spices, and extracts.

SANGUIGNI PASTA, INC.
6707 East McKellips Road
Mesa, AR 85215
(480) 654-1054
Fine pastas mailed around the country.

TODARO BROTHERS
555 2nd Avenue
New York, NY 10016
(212) 532-0633
Imported Italian mozzarella, Parmigiano, fresh, dried, and frozen pastas, meats, vegetables, and more.

URBANI USA
2924 40th Avenue
Long Island City, NY 11101
(718) 392-5050
www.urbani.com
Importers of fine Italian truffles (white and black), porcini mushrooms (fresh or frozen, as well as dried), truffle oil, bottarga, and more.

VIAREGGIO ITALIAN GROCERY & DELI
1727 Connecticut Avenue N.W.
Washington, D.C. 20009
(202) 332-9100
Delicious homemade pastas, sauces, Italian gourmet items, wines, and exceptional produce.

Patrizio Siddu's pennoni with
sausage, arugula, and balsamic
vinegar (recipe on page 175),
ideal on a winter night.

index

signature
pasta